LEARN
CHINESE
(HÀNYǓ)
THE FAST AND FUN WAY

by Lifei Ji

To help you pace your learning, we've included
stopwatches *like the one above* throughout
the book to mark each 15-minute interval.
You can read one of these units each day
or pace yourself according to your needs.

BARRON'S

All inquiries should be addressed to:
Barron's Educational Series, Inc.
250 Wireless Boulevard
Hauppauge, New York 11788

International Standard Book No. 0-8120-9689-4

Library of Congress Catalog Card No. 97-73483

Printed in the United States of America
9 8 7 6 5 4 3 2

CONTENTS

Introduction *1*
Pronunciation Guide *2*
How English and Chinese Are
Different and How They Are
Similar *6*

GETTING TO KNOW PEOPLE *7*
1   Let's Talk *7*

ARRIVAL *15*
2   Where to Spend the Night *15*

SEEING THE SIGHTS *21*
3   How to Get There (on Foot) *21*
4   Public Transportation *26*
5   Time and Numbers *30*
6   On the Train *42*
7   Countries and Languages *46*
8   On the Road *51*
9   Camping *62*
10 Seasons of the Year, Months, Weather,
    Days of the Week *67*
11 Airplanes *73*

ENTERTAINMENT *79*
12 Theater, Movies, Holidays *79*
13 Sport(s) *85*

ORDERING A MEAL *89*
14 Breakfast, Lunch, Dinner *89*
15 The Restaurant/Tips *94*

HOW ARE WE DOING? *99*

AT THE STORE *104*
16 Clothing, Sizes, Colors *104*
17 Food Stores/Weights/Costs *110*
18 Drugstore/Pharmacy *116*
19 Laundry/Dry Cleaner's *122*
20 Beauty Salon/Barber Shop *126*
21 The Newsstand/Stationery Goods/
    Office Supplies *131*
22 Jewelry/Watches *135*
23 Gifts, Souvenirs, Records *140*
24 Repair Services: Eyeglasses, Shoes *146*

ESSENTIAL SERVICES *149*
25 Bank *149*
26 Mail/Post Office *155*
27 Telephone *159*
28 Doctor, Dentist, Hospital *162*
29 Help! *172*

BEFORE YOU LEAVE *175*

VOCABULARY CARDS *185*

CHINESE-ENGLISH AND
ENGLISH-CHINESE DICTIONARY
Special Section: Food and Drink Guide,
    Tips on Tipping

For my daughter, Ke Ji, and all my American friends.

With gratitude to my wife for her loving support of my writing.

INTRODUCTION

Everything in China seems larger than life. This country has the world's largest population, with more than one billion people. Its long history, its culture, and its civilization go back thousands of years. China's vast area covers more than 3,690,000 square miles, making it the third largest in the world. It is bounded by Afghanistan, Bhutan, Burma, India, Kazakhstan, North Korea, Kyrgyzstan, Laos, Macau, Mongolia, Nepal, Pakistan, Russia, Tajikistan, and Vietnam. The climate of China is extremely diverse, tropical in the south to subarctic in the north.

It is not very long since China opened its door to welcome visitors to her splendid historical sites and impressive scenic spots. The Himalayas along China's southwestern frontier, the world's tallest mountains, are the final challenge to mountain climbers. The Changjiang River, the world's fourth longest, offers magnificent scenery. The Taklimakan Desert, one of the driest spots on Earth, challenges anybody to conquer it. The Great Wall, the only man-built object on Earth that can be seen from outer space, is 1,400 miles long, was in place long before Rome became an empire, and begs to be photographed.

歡迎您! Welcome!

Beijing, the capital of the nation, is a fascinating city with modern highways and narrow streets weaving together between the modern skyscrapers and ancient oriental quadrangles. Beijing is centered around the Forbidden City and Tiananmen Square, the world's biggest public square. You will need a whole day just to see the important attractions around it. They include the Museum of the Chinese Revolution and Chinese History; the Qianmen Gate; the Monument to the People's Heroes and Mao's Memorial Hall; the Great Hall of the People, seat of China's Congress; and Tiananmen Gate (Gate of Heavenly Peace), where China's leaders stand on national days to review the parades and festivities. Beijing is the political, cultural, and economic center of China. Thus, the city provides a great variety of sightseeing and entertainment opportunities. It is also a gourmet's delight, with excellent food from all over China and the world.

China has very good public transportation systems. In big cities like Beijing, you can go almost anywhere by city bus. National transportation by air, water, or land is also excellent.

The Chinese people have shared a common culture longer than any other group on Earth. The writing system, for example, dates back 4,000 years. Today, one in every five people on Earth speaks Chinese.

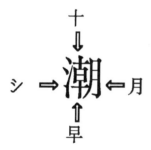

Now you have the opportunity to join this enormous community and to enjoy the advantages and the pleasure of knowing the basics of the Chinese language. Welcome!

PRONUNCIATION GUIDE

The basic sounds of modern Chinese are not difficult to reproduce if you speak English. Take a few minutes to study and practice this Pronunciation Guide, and you will be able to follow this book and sound like a Chinese.

Pinyin (spelling the sounds of Chinese characters) uses the English alphabet. Most of the letters are similar to the English sounds. Only a few sounds in modern Chinese do not occur in English. Most Chinese syllables consist of two parts: an initial (beginning sound) and a final (ending sound).

Initials (Beginning Sounds)

1. Most syllables begin with a consonant, and some with a vowel. The following Chinese initials have the same pronunciation as English. Pronounce them as you would English.

Chinese Initials	Description of Sound	Example
b	as in *book*	bù = no
d	as in *dad*	dà = big
f	as in *fork*	fù = rich
g	as *good*	guó = country
h	as in *horse*	huà = picture
j	as in *jeep*	jìjié = season
k	as in *kite*	kàn = look
l	as in *look*	lìliàng = strength
m	as in *moon*	míng = bright
n	as in *noon*	nín = you
p	as in *paper*	pà = afraid
s	as in *see*	sùdù = speed
t	as in *tea*	tàipíng = peace

2. The following initials are different than they are in English, but the closest sound can be found in English.

Chinese initials	Description of Sound	Example
c	like *ts* in i*ts*	cí-bēi = kind
q	like *ch* in *ch*ip	qiángdà = powerful
x	like *sh* in *sh*eep	xiàoyuán = campus
z	like *ds* in han*ds*	zàijiàn = good-bye

2

3. The following retracted initials do not exist in English and need special attention.

Chinese initials	Description of Sound	Example
r	like *r* in *r*ule when it is before *u* or *-ong*; otherwise, it sounds like the *s* in plea*s*ure.	Rùmén = elementary course róngyì = easy rè = hot rén = man, person
ch	like *ts* in i*ts*, but with tongue retracted (the tip of the tongue turned up and back to touch the roof of the mouth)	chī = eat
sh	like *s* in *s*ee, but with tongue retracted	shì = yes
zh	like *ds* in han*ds*, but with tongue retracted	zhànghù = account

Finals (Ending Sounds)

The element after the initial in a Chinese syllable is the final sound. Some Chinese words end in only one vowel (Simple Finals), some in two or three vowels, and some in nasal sounds like -n or -ng (Compound Finals).

1. Simple Finals
There are six simple finals:

Chinese Pinyin finals	Description of Sound	Example
a	as in *f*a*ther, with the mouth open	bàba = daddy, father
o	like *aw* in s*aw*	bóbo = uncle
e	like *u* in c*u*p but after *y* like the *e* in y*e*s	cèsuǒ = bathroom, toilet yě = also
i	as in sk*i*, except after *c, ch, r, s, sh, z, zh*, when it is like the *i* in s*i*r	dìtú = map chī = eat shì = yes
u	like the *u* in s*u*per, except after *j, q, x, y*, when it is like *ü*	dúshū = read jùjí = gather qù = go
ü	sound made with tongue in position of *i* (sk*i*) with lips rounded	nǚ rén = woman

2. Compound Finals

Chinese Pinyin	Description of Sound	Example
ai	as in *ai*sle or the *i* in b*i*ke	dài = wear
an	like the *a* in f*a*ther plus the *n* in i*n*	kàn = look
ang	like the *a* in f*a*ther plus the *ng* in lo*ng*	dāngxīn = Be careful.
ao	like the *ow* in n*ow*	dàoqiè = steal
ou	like the *o* in h*o*me	dōu = all
ong	like the *aw* in s*aw* plus *ng* in lo*ng*	dòngwù = animal
ei	as in *ei*ght	hēi = black
en	like the *un* in *un*der	hèn = hate
eng	like the *ung* in l*ung*	lěng = cold
er	as in t*erm*	értóng = child, children
ia	like the *ya* in *ya*cht	jiā = family, home
ie	like the *e* in y*e*t	jiérì = holiday
iao	start with *ee* in s*ee* and end with *ow* in n*ow*	jiàotáng = church
in	as in t*in*	jìnlái = come in, enter
ing	as in s*ing*	jīngjù = Beijing opera
ian	like *yen*	jiǎnpiào = check in
ua	like the *u* in p*u*t plus the *a* in f*a*ther	guà = hang
uo	like the *u* in p*u*t plus the *aw* in s*aw*	guó = country
uai	like *why*	guài = odd, strange
un	like the *u* in p*u*t plus the *n* in fu*n*	kùn = sleepy
ün	start with tongue in position of *i* (i*nn*) with lips rounded and end in -*n*	yún = cloud

Tones

Every syllable in modern Chinese, theoretically speaking, has four tones. Like the initial and the final, the tone is part of a syllable. The tone can drastically alter the syllable's meaning. For example, the sound "ma" with four different tones has four different meanings.

mā means "mother"
má means "hemp"
mǎ means "horse"
mà means "to scold"

Let's take a look at an another example.

dī means "low"
dí means "enemy"
dǐ means "bottom"
dì means "brother"

Nà shì wǒde mǎ.

The tone is the variation of the speaker's pitch. It does not change with one's emotion English. To get a feel of how the four tones sound, try to say "no" in these four different way

No. Strike a high note as you say no, keeping the tone pitched high and level (1st tone).
No? Say no as if you were questioning, raising your voice sharply (2nd tone).
N-o. Say no as if you were doubting, stretching the word to a lower pitch (3rd tone).
No! Say no as if you were angry or impatient, with the tone falling sharply (4th tone).

The diagram below illustrates the range of the variation of one's pitch while four different tones are produced. In the first tone the voice stays level but at a high pitch. The second tone starts in the middle register and rises to the high. The third tone starts at a middle-low level and falls to low. The fourth tone falls sharply from high to low.

1 = high

2 = middle-high

3 = middle

4 = middle-low

5 = low

(ˉ) 1st tone ———the high tone: 1 → 1
(´) 2nd tone———the rising tone: 3 → 5
(ˇ) 3rd tone———the low tone: 4 → 5 → 5
(`) 4th tone ———the falling tone: 1 → 5

Other Important Rules for Spelling and Pronunciation:

1. In writing, *w* is used for a word whose sound begins with the vowel *u* (as, u → wu, ua → wa, uai → wai); *y* is used for *i*, or *ü* (as, i → yi, ü → yu, üe → yue).

2. The dots above *ü* are dropped when it is preceded by *j, q, x,* or *y* (as, ju, qu, xu, xun, yuan).

3. In writing, *iu* is a short form for *iou*, and *ui* for *uei*.

4. In writing, tone marks (ˉ ´ ˇ `) are on the main vowel, the one pronounced the loudest and with the mouth open widest. Examples: *guó* = country, *jiǎn-piào* = check in, *jié-rì* = holiday.

5. In a sentence or a phrase, some words do not carry their tone marks because they are unstressed in that group of words. Examples: the word *bù* (= *no*, or *not*) is unstressed in the phrase *Duìbuqǐ* (=*Excuse me*, or *Sorry*).

6. When two third tones are in succession, the first one changes into a rising tone, the second tone.
Examples: Nǐ hǎo → Ní hǎo! (Hello!)
shǒu biǎo → shóu biǎo (watch)

HOW ENGLISH AND CHINESE ARE DIFFERENT AND HOW THEY ARE SIMILAR
中英文的不同與相同

Looking at the title above, you may wonder how in the world Chinese and English are similar. We can almost be sure that they are different. One is spelled out in the Roman alphabet; the other is written in characters. Well, there are some similarities between the two languages. The pinyin system, which was officially adopted by China in 1953, has successfully Romanized the Chinese language, and thus made it possible for English-speaking people to learn Chinese in the fast and fun way.

Moreover, the English and Chinese languages share some basic grammar rules. A sentence has a subject and a predicate; the word order is pretty much the same. Notice the differences and similarities in the following examples.

Group 1

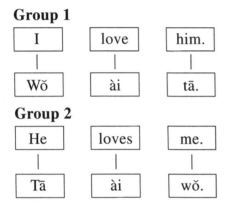

Group 2

The change of the word order changes the meaning in both English and Chinese. From the 1st group to the 2nd group, English has to make all the necessary changes for its pronouns and verbs. (*him* → *He*; *love* → *loves*; *I* → *me*). But Chinese has the same pronouns (*ta* and *wo*) for both subject and object. And the verbs do not have special forms for the third person singular or even for the different tenses. Examples:

Group 1

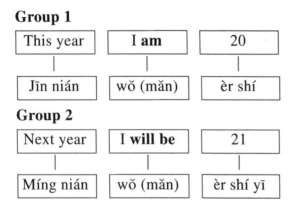

Group 2

In Chinese, you really don't have to worry about the prefixes or suffixes for the Chinese words because they do not exist in the language. In this sense, Chinese is easier, isn't it?

As you go on with this book, you will find Chinese is not as hard to learn as you thought. I am glad you have gone this far. Keep up the good work. Just take it easy, 15 minutes a day. It's the fast and fun way!

GETTING TO KNOW PEOPLE

Jiéshí Rénmen

1	**Huìhuà**
	Let's Talk

Knowing some basic Chinese expressions will be helpful when you first arrive in China. The following dialogues deal with expressions that are needed to meet people and to ask for help. Read the dialogues aloud several times. More practice will make the difference.

Mark Smith, his wife, Mary, their son, Paul, and their daughter, Anne, have just arrived at the Beijing International Airport. They've claimed their luggage and gone through customs. Now they want to find the bus for downtown. They approach a porter.

MARK	**Duìbuqǐ.....**	Excuse me...
PORTER	**Yǒu shìma?**	May I help you?
MARK	**Qǐng wèn jìn chéng zài nǎr dā chē?**	Where do we take the bus for downtown, please?
PORTER	**Jiù zài nèibiān.**	It's right over there.
MARK	**Xièxie.**	Thank you.

On the bus downtown, Mark strikes up a conversation with Wang Gang, a Chinese man sitting next to him.

MARK	**Ní hǎo. Wǒ jiào Mǎkè Shǐmìsī.**	Hello. My name is Mark Smith.
WANG	**Ní hǎo, Shǐmìsī Xiānsheng.**	Hello, Mr. Smith.
MARK	**Nín jiào shénme?**	What's your name?
WANG	**Wǒ jiào Wáng Gāng.**	I'm Wang Gang.
MARK	**Hěn gāoxìng rènshi nín.**	Nice to meet you.
WANG	**Nín shì nǎ guó rén?**	Where are you from?
MARK	**Wǒ shì měiguó rén. Zhè shì wǒmen yì jiā. Wǒ tàitai, érzi hé nǚér.**	I'm from the United States. This is my family—my wife, my son, and my daughter.
WANG	**Nǐmen hǎo. Hěn gāoxìng rènshi nǐmen.**	Hi, nice to meet you.

About an hour later, the bus arrives in downtown Beijing. Mr. Wang helps the Smiths with their luggage to their hotel and then they say good-bye.

WANG	**Dào le nínde bīnguǎn.**	Here we are, at your hotel.
MARK	**Fēicháng gǎnxiè.**	Thank you very much.
WANG	**Búyòngxiè.**	You're welcome.
MARK	**Zàijiàn.**	Good-bye.
WANG	**Zàijiàn.**	Good-bye.

Now, match the Chinese expressions with their English equivalents. Try not to look at the dialogues.

1. **Búyòngxiè.**		a.	Excuse me...
2. **Dào le.**		b.	Good-bye.
3. **Duìbuqǐ.....**		c.	Hello.
4. **Hěn gāo xìng rèn shi nǐmen.**		d.	Here we are.
5. **Ní hǎo.**		e.	May I help you?
6. **Nín jiào shén me?**		f.	My name is...
7. **Nín shì nǎ guó rén?**		g.	Nice to meet you.
8. **Wǒ jiào _____ .**		h.	Thank you.
9. **Xièxie.**		i.	This is my family.
10. **Yǒu shì ma?**		j.	What's your name?
11. **Zàijiàn.**		k.	Where are you from?
12. **Zhè shì wǒmen yì jiā.**		l.	You're welcome.

Rén yǔ Wù

People and Things

When speaking any language, you need to build up your vocabulary, especially nouns. In our everyday life we encounter different people and various things. In Chinese, nouns are easier to learn than in English because you don't have to worry about their singular or plural forms.

Let's take a look at the following examples:

bǐ
a pen

bǐ
pens

Wǒ yǒu yì zhī bǐ.
I have a pen.

Wǒ yǒu jǐ zhī bǐ.
I have some pens.

Now read the following nouns and write them in the space provided.

shū
a book, books

1. _____

fángzi
a house, houses

2. _____

shù
a tree, trees

3. _____

jiǎo
foot, feet

4. _____

You have just looked at nouns designating inanimate objects. Here are some words for people. Note in Chinese there is a word—"men"—that can be used after each noun denoting people to show plurals. But you don't have to use it in everyday Chinese, only when you address your audience formally. Example: "Nǚshìmen, xiānshēngmen" (Ladies and Gentlemen).

háizi
child

háizi (men)
children

nánhái
boy

nánhái (men)
boys

nǚhái
girl

nǚhái (men)
girls

māma
mother

māma (men)
mothers

Write these nouns in the spaces provided.

1. boy/boys   _____   _____

2. child/children   _____   _____

3. girl/girls   _____   _____

4. mother/mothers   _____   _____

10

Dazhaohu yu Chengwèi
Greetings and Names

Nowadays, Chinese people greet each other in almost the same way as Americans do. In the morning, they say "Good morning!" of course in Chinese, and "Good night" when departing at night. Let's look at the common greetings below:

Zǎoshang hǎo.	Good morning.
Xiàwǔ hǎo.	Good afternoon.
Wǎnshang hǎo.	Good evening.
Nín hǎo.	Hello/Hi.
Wǎn ān.	Good night.

English-speaking people, especially Americans like to greet people with "How are you (doing)?" The answer is almost always "I'm (doing) fine." no matter whether he or she is really fine or not. For Chinese people "How are you?" is not a greeting but a question.

Similarly, a common Chinese greeting **"Nǐ chī le ma?"**(meaning "Hello/Hi"), still used in some parts of China may sound strange to English speakers if literally translated (Literally, *Have you eaten [your meal]?*).

Now, how would you greet someone at 9 A.M.?   **1.** _____
at 2 P.M.?   **2.** _____
at 8 P.M.?   **3.** _____

In China, people introduce themselves more or less the same way as Americans do. It's natural to start a friendly conversation by asking each other's names. However, Chinese names are quite different from English ones. Notice the following differences:

Family (Last) Names Go First
Most Chinese names consist of two or three characters or syllables, such as *Wang Gang, Wang Xin Gang*. Chinese family (last) names go first, and the given (first) names last. So *Wang Gang* or *Wang Xin Gang* should be addressed as Mr. Wang (**Wáng Xiānsheng**).

A Married Woman Keeps Her Own Family Name
Don't be surprised when you see a married couple with two different family names. In China, family names are very important. A woman keeps her family name even after she is married.

ANSWERS
Note: *Nín hǎo is an acceptable answer for all three questions.*
1. Zǎoshang hǎo.   2. Xiàwǔ hǎo.   3. Wǎnshang hǎo.

11

Xiǎo & Lǎo (Young and Old)

Among colleagues at workplaces or among friends, the younger ones would be called either by their full names or by *Xiǎo* + his or her family name. *Xiǎo* means "Junior" or "young." The older would be called by their proper title + family names or by *Lǎo* + family names. *Lǎo* means "Senior" or "Old"; please keep in mind that China is a country where the elderly are respected.

First Names

Unlike American first names, Chinese given names (first names) are rarely used. They are used only
  • by parents for their children,
  • by the elder members for the younger ones in a family, and
  • by very close friends.

Tánlùn Jiātíng Chéngyuán
Let's Talk about the Family

Unlike English, Chinese has a word for every family member, which indicates his or her relationship in the family. Take grandparents for example. Grandfather can be both father's father or mother's father in English. But in Chinese, *yéye* refers to father's father; *wàigōng* refers to mother's father. Study the most common words for family members in the following lists.

List #1

	Father's Side	Mother's Side
grandfather	**yéye**	**wàigōng**
grandmother	**nǎinai**	**wàipó**
uncle	**bóbo** (older than father)	
	shūshu (younger than father)	**jiùjiu**
aunt	**gūmǔ**	**yímǔ**

List #2

father	**bàba**
mother	**mā ma**
brother	**gē ge** (older than you)
	dì di (younger than you)
sister	**jiě jie** (older than you)
	mèi mei (younger than you)
cousin	**táng + gē, dì, jiě, or mèi**
	biǎo + gē, dì, jiě or mèi
	[Note *táng* here indicates cousins who have the same *yéye* (grandfather, [father's father]); *biǎo* refers to the rest of the cousins.]
nephew	**zhízi** (brother's son)
	wàishēng (sister's son)
niece	**zhínǚ** (brother's daughter)
	wàishēngnǚ (sister's daughter)

I. Now say the right word for the following. Look at the lists if you need to.

1. father's father _____

2. mother's father _____

3. father's mother _____

4. mother's mother _____

5. father's brother _____

6. mother's brother _____

7. father's sister _____

8. mother's sister _____

9. the son of one's father's brother _____

II. Match the Chinese with the English meaning.

1. gēge   a. niece (sister's daughter)

2. dìdi   b. brother (younger than you)

3. jiějie   c. sister (older than you)

4. mèimei   d. niece (brother's daughter)

5. zhízi   e. sister (younger than you)

6. wàishēng   f. nephew (brother's son)

7. zhínǚ   g. brother (older than you)

8. wàishēgnǚ   h. nephew (sister's son)

13

Look at the Chinese words below for an apartment. Repeat each of the words several times and then practice writing them in the spaces below.

Gōngyù
An Apartment

chúfáng
kitchen

mén
door

guànxǐshì
bathroom

bīngxiāng
refrigerator

zǎopén
bathtub

kǎoxiāng
oven

shuǐchí
sink

kètīng
living room

wòshì
bedroom

shāfā
sofa

bìchú
closet

zhuōzi
table

yǐzi
chair

zǒuláng
hallway

chuānghu
window

chuáng
bed

ARRIVAL
Dǐdá

You'll probably already have booked a room from home—either in a hotel or with a private family—at least for your first few days in China. In fact, unless you have been invited by someone who will arrange for your accommodations, you should not leave home without a reservation. Even so, you'll want to know some basic words and phrases that describe the services and facilities you can expect to find. Learn these words first, and notice how they are used in the dialogues you will read later.

bīnguǎn
hotel

kèfáng
hotel room

huāfèi
cost

guànxǐshì
bathroom

línyù
shower

yùdìng
to reserve

jiēdàiyuán
hotel clerk

guǎnlǐyuán
administrator

fúwùyuán
maid

hùzhào
passport

yàoshi
key

diàntī
elevator

Duōshǎo?
How Much/Many?

The numbers are absolutely essential if you wish to get by in Chinese. Take a look and try to pronounce the following numbers from one to ten. Then practice your writing in the spaces supplied.

Number	Chinese	
0	líng	_____
1	yī	_____
2	èr	_____
3	sān	_____
4	sì	_____
5	wǔ	_____
6	liù	_____
7	qī	_____
8	bā	_____
9	jiǔ	_____
10	shí	_____

Let's see if you can fill in the blanks after the numerals with their correct names. Solve the problems along the way. Note: Plus is **jiā**, Minus is **jiǎn**, Equals is **děngyú**.

1. 2 _____ + (jiā)   3 _____ = **děngyú** _____
2. 5 _____ + (jiā)   2 _____ = **děngyú** _____
3. 6 _____ + (jiā)   4 _____ = **děngyú** _____
4. 8 _____ − (jiǎn) 7 _____ = **děngyú** _____
5. 9 _____ − (jiǎn) 6 _____ = **děngyú** _____

Kèfáng
A Hotel Room

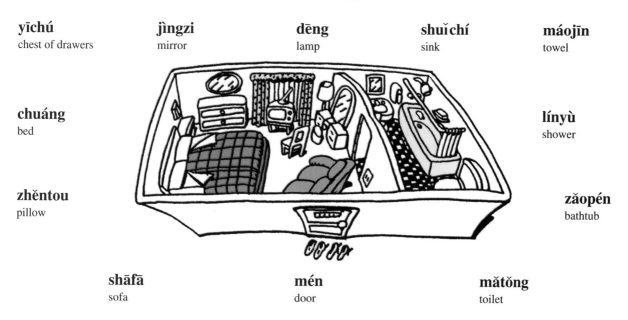

yīchú chest of drawers	**jìngzi** mirror	**dēng** lamp	**shuǐchí** sink	**máojīn** towel
chuáng bed				**línyù** shower
zhěntou pillow				**zǎopén** bathtub
	shāfā sofa	**mén** door	**mǎtǒng** toilet	

Zěnyàng Tíwèn
How to Ask Questions

When you are traveling, you will need to ask a lot of questions. For questions that can be answered with yes or no, it is easy. Just put the word **"ma"** at the end of the sentence and raise your voice toward the end of the sentence the way you would in English.

Tā gāng dào.   He or she has just arrived.
Tā gāng dào ma?   Has he or she just arrived?

Nǐ è le.   You are hungry.
Nǐ è le ma?   Are you hungry?

For other types of questions, get familiar with these words.

Chinese word	English
shuí	Who
héshí/shéme shíhòu	When
hédì/nǎr	Where
shénme	What
zěnyàng	How
duōshǎo	How much, how many

Now make the following sentences into questions.

1. **Zhè shì wǒde hùzhào.**
   This is my passport.

   Is this my passport?

2. **Tāmen zài zhèr yùdìng le fángjiān.**
   They have a reservation here.

   Do they have a reservation here?

3. **Jīntiān shì xīngqīwǔ.**
   Today is Friday.

   Is today Friday?

Now for some more adventures of the Smith family as they check into their hotel. Look at the words carefully and then try to read them aloud to practice your pronunciation.

MARK   **Ní hǎo.**   Hello.

                   Wǒmen wèi jīntiān yùdìng   We reserved two rooms for today.

                   le liǎng gè fángjiān.

ANSWERS

3. Jīntiān shì xīngqī wǔ ma?

1. Zhè shì wǒde hùzhào ma?   2. Tāmen zài zhèr yùdìng le fángjiān ma?

CLERK	Zǎoshàng hǎo.	Good morning.
	Nín xìng shénme?	What's your last name?
MARK	Wǒ xìng Shǐmìsī.	My name is Smith.
CLERK	Duì, Shǐmìsī Xiānsheng.	Yes, Mr. Smith.
	Wǒmen yǒu nínde yùdìng	We have your reservation.
	jìlù. Qǐng tiánhǎo zhè	Would you fill out this form?
	zhāng dānzi.	
MARK	Hǎo de.	Yes.
CLERK	Qǐngwèn, nínde hùzhào ne?	May I have your passport, please?
MARK	Zài zhèr.	Here you are.
CLERK	Nín jiāng zài wǒmen zhèr	How long will you be staying
	dāi duōjiǔ?	with us?
MARK	Dàyuē yì xīngqī.	About a week.
CLERK	Hǎode.	All right.
MARK	Fángjià bāokuò zǎocān ma?	Is breakfast included in the price
		of the room?
CLERK	Bù bāokuò. Búguò wǒmende	No, it isn't. But we have a nice
	kāfēidiàn bú cuò.	coffee shop.
MARK	Wǒ zhīdao le.	I see.
CLERK	Nínde fángjiān zài liù lóu.	Your rooms are on the sixth floor.
	Nínde yàoshi zài zhèr.	Here are your keys.
MARK	Xièxie. Diàntī zài nǎr?	Thank you. Where is the elevator?
CLERK	Yìzhí zǒu, ránhòu wǎng	Go straight ahead, and then to
	yòu guǎi.	the right.
MARK	Fēicháng gǎnxiè.	Thank you very much.
CLERK	Búkèqi.	You're welcome.

After you have reviewed the dialogue a few times, see if you can fill in the blanks with the correct Chinese words.

1. **Nín xìng** _____ ?
   (What's your last name?)

2. _____, nínde hùzhào ne?
   (May I have your passport, please?)

3. **Nín jiāng zài wǒmen zhèr dāi** _____ ?
   (How long will you be staying with us?)

4. **Fángjià bāokuò zǎocān** _____ ?
   (Is breakfast included in the price of the room?)

5. **Diàntī zài** _____ ?
   (Where is the elevator?)

"Magic Words"

Being polite and well-mannered is always welcomed and appreciated everywhere. Let's learn a few little "magic" words that will make your trip a little easier.

Xièxie.	**Qǐng.**	**Búkèqi.**
Thank you.	Please.	You're welcome.

In the maze below, find the Chinese words for *please, thank you, you're welcome, passport, key, hotel,* and *maid.*

```
N  B  B  H  N  B  Y  K  G  L
Z  A  N  R  B  B  F  N  P  W
F  O  U  A  O  U  I  J  M  Y
U  P  A  G  U  Q  K  O  A  I
E  Y  G  H  N  Y  E  E  L  M
Q  L  A  S  Z  I  U  J  Q  Y
Y  B  A  O  X  U  B  W  F  I
P  U  Z  E  S  F  H  G  U  E
X  F  I  C  N  H  P  E  F  F
I  Z  D  F  M  T  I  J  C  O
```

SEEING THE SIGHTS
Guānguāng

3	**Bùxíng**
	(How to Get There) on Foot

"How do I get to . . . ?" "Where is the nearest subway?" "Is the museum straight ahead?" You'll be asking directions and getting answers wherever you travel. Get to know the words and phrases that will make getting around easier. Study the new words and say them aloud several times. Make sure you understand them.

jiēdào
street

guǎngchǎng
square

yìzhí
straight

Mary and Mark have just left their hotel for their first morning of sight-seeing.

Although they have a map of the city, they decide to try out their new Chinese skills and ask the policeman on the corner for directions.

kào zuǒbiān
to the left

MARK (to policeman)
Qǐngwèn, qù bówùguǎn zěnme zǒu?
Excuse me, how can we get to the museum?

yóujú
post ofice

kào yòubiān
to the right

POLICEMAN (Jǐngchá)
Yán zhè tiáo jiē zǒu.
Go along this street.

shízìlùkǒu
intersection

Dào hónglǜdēng, xiàng zuǒ guǎi.
To the traffic light. Turn left.

hónglǜdēng
traffic light

Ránhòu, zǒu dào xiàyígè shízìlùkǒu, xiàng yòu guǎi.
Then go to the next intersection. You turn right.

Zài xiàng qián zǒu yìdiǎnr. Bówùguǎn jiù zài nǐ zuǒbiān.
Go a little farther. The museum is on your left.

MARY   **Xièxie.**
Thank you.

POLICEMAN   **Búkèqi.**
You're welcome.

Wǒmen Zài Nǎr?
Where Are We?

zhuōzi _____
table

māo _____
cat

Let's learn the words and phrases to describe locations.

zài . . . hòumian
behind

zài . . . qiánmian
in front of

zài . . . shàngmian
on

zài . . . xiàmian
under

jǐnāizhe . . .
next to

. . . fùjìn
near

Now take a look at the **nánhái** (boy) and the **fángzi** (house). Can you write in the proper words to locate him?

1. _____

2. _____

3. _____

4. _____

5. _____

6. _____

Zhè Háishì Nà

This or That

Let's learn to say **zhè** (this) or **nà** (that). You can use your finger as you would in English to point to things near you and say **zhè,** or say **nà** for those far away. Try to respond to the following questions and fill in the blanks with your answers.

1. **Nín xǐhuān zhè ge háishì nà ge?**
   Would you like this one or that one?

   _____ ge.
   This one, please.

2. **Nǐ ná de zhè ge háishì nà ge?**
   Did you take this one or that one?

   Wǒ ná de _____ ge.
   I took that one.

23

Chángyòng Cí
Some Useful Words

Write the Chinese words in the space provided and say them aloud.

diànyǐngyuàn
movie theater
_____

shāngdiàn
store
_____

yínháng
bank
_____

jiàotáng
church
_____

jiēdào
street
_____

qìchē
car
_____

yàodiàn
pharmacy
_____

bàotān
kiosk
_____

Bùxíng Lái Qù
Coming and Going (on Foot)

Chinese verbs do not have to change forms to agree with their subjects, nor do they change for the tenses. Look at the following examples.

wǒ qù	_____	I am going.../go
nǐ qù	_____	you are going.../go
tā qù	_____	he or she is going.../goes
wǒmen qù	_____	we are going.../go
nǐmen qù	_____	you are going.../go
tāmen qù	_____	they are going.../go

Năr?

"Where?" (to Be Put)

You have already learned how to make a yes-or-no question by simply putting the "**ma**" at the end of a sentence.

For questions like Where, Who, What, How, etc., Chinese use these special question words in the place where the answer is supposed to be in a sentence.

Example:

Tā	qù	Zhōngguó.
He	is going to	China.

Tā	qù	năr?
He	is going	where?

More examples:

Tā	măi le	yì běn shū.
She	bought	a book.

Tā	măi le	shénme?
She	bought	what?

Tāmen	míngtiān	líkāi.
They	tomorrow	leave.

Tāmen	shénme shíhòu	líkāi?
They	when	leave?

Now let's try to ask questions about the underlined parts, using **shuí** (who), **shénme shíhòu** (when), **hédì/năr** (where), **shénme** (what), and **duōshăo** (how much, how many).

1. <u>Tāmen</u> zài zhèr yùdìng le fángjiān. _____?
   <u>They</u> have reserved a room/rooms here.

2. Tamen zài <u>zhèr</u> yùdìng le fángjian. _____?
   They have reserved a room/rooms <u>here</u>.

3. Tāmen zài zhèr yùdìng le <u>fángjiān</u>. _____?
   They have reserved <u>a room/rooms</u> here.

4. Tā <u>zuótiān</u> măi le sì běn shū. _____?
   She bought four books <u>yesterday</u>.

5. Tā zuótian măi le <u>sì</u> běn shū. _____?
   She bought <u>four</u> books yesterday.

ANSWERS

1. Shuí zài zhè yùdìng le fángjiān?   2. Tamen zài năr yùdìng le fángjiān?   3. Tāmen zài zhè yùdìng le shénme?   4. Tā shénme shíhòu măi le sì běn shū?   5. Tā zuótiān măi le duōshăo běn shū?

25

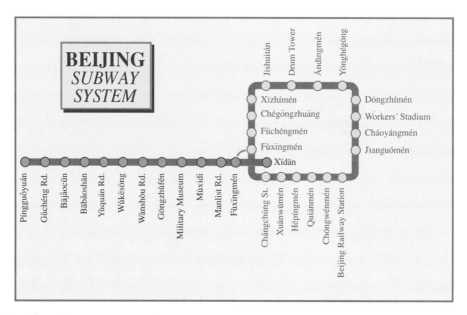

The following dialogue contains some words and expressions you will find useful when using public transportation. Read the dialogue aloud several times to familiarize yourself with the meaning and pronunciation of the words.

MARY	**Wǒmen zuò chūzū qìchē qù jùyuàn ba.**	Let's take a taxi to the theater.
MARK	**Bùxíng. Nà tài guì le.**	No. That's too expensive.
MARY	**Zuò dìtiě xíng ma?**	How about the subway?
	Yòu shūshì yòu kuài.	That's both comfortable and quick.
MARK	**Duì. Kěshì nǐ shénme yě kànbújiàn.**	Yes. But you can't see anything.
MARY	**Nà jiù zuò gōnggòngqìchē ba.**	Well, then let's take the bus.

Zài gōnggòngqìche shàng (on the bus).

MARK	**Qǐngwèn, piàojià shì duōshao?**	Excuse me, how much is the fare?
DRIVER	**Yí kuài qián.**	One yuan.
MARK	**Wǒmen xiǎng zài Běijīng jùyuàn fùjìn xià che.**	We want to get off near the Beijing Theater.
DRIVER	**Dào shí wǒ gàosu nǐmen.**	I'll tell you when we get there.
MARK	**Fēicháng gǎnxiè.**	Thank you very much.

Now circle the best answer, according to the dialogue.

1. **Tāmen yào qù nǎli?** (Where were they going?)
   Tāmen yào qù _____.
   a. **Bēijīng jùyuàn**   b. **guǎngchǎng**   c. **shāngdiàn**

2. **Tāmen shì zěnyàng qù jùyuàn de?** (How did they go to the theater?)
   Tāmen shì _____ qù jùyuàn de.
   a. **chéng dìtie**   b. **chéng chūzūqìchē**   c. **chéng gōnggòngqìchē**

3. **Piàojià shì duōshǎo?** (How much is the fare?)
   Piàojià shì _____.
   a. **yí kuài qián**   b. **sān kuài qián**   c. **sì kuài qián**

In spoken Chinese, we use "**zùo**" to mean "take (a vehicle)." Look at the pictures below, repeat the phrases, and then write them in the blanks.

zùo chūzūqìchē

_____

zùo gōnggòngqìchē

_____

zùo dìtiě

_____

zùo chē

_____

ANSWERS

1.a   2.c   3.a

Here are some more phrases to help you communicate with the bus conductor.

shàngchē	to get on, to ride in
xiàchē	to get off
huànchē	to transfer
yìngbì	coins
chēzhàn	bus stop
shòupiàoyuán	bus conductor
sījī	bus driver

Shuí de/Shéi de

Whose?

You may notice that "whose" in Chinese is shuí (who) + de (structural particle). Actually, a noun or a pronoun can also be used the same way to show possession. Let's first take a look at the personal pronouns used in this way.

ENGLISH	CHINESE	CLOSE LOOK
My	**wǒde**	wǒ (I) + de
Your	**nǐde**	nǐ (you) + de
Her/His	**tāde**	tā (she/he) + de
Our	**wǒmende**	wǒmen (we) + de
Your	**nǐmende**	nǐmen (you) + de
Their	**tāmende**	tāmen (they) + de

Let's go on to look at some examples of nouns used in this way.

teacher's	**lǎoshīde**	lǎoshī (teacher) + de
American	**Měiguóde**	Měiguó (America) + de
Chinese	**Zhōngguóde**	Zhōngguó (China) + de
... of the hotel	**bīnguǎnde**	bīnguǎn (hotel) + de

The interrogative word may be used to raise a question and it is placed where the answer is expected. Examples:

Tā shì <u>shuí de</u> lǎoshi?   (Whose teacher is he?)

Tā shì <u>wǒde</u> lǎoshi.   (He is my teacher.)

Now fill in the blanks according to the English:

1. _____ **māo**   (my cat)

2. _____ **jiě**   (their street)

3. _____ **gǒu**   (our dog)

4. _____ **zhuōzi**   (her table)

5. _____ **yéye** (your grandfather)

6. _____ **yínháng**   (your *pl.* bank)

7. **Zhè shì** _____ **hùzhào?**   (Whose passport is this?)

8. **Nà shì** _____ **hùzhào.**   (It's grandfather's passport.)

Duōshǎo

How Much/Many?

The numbers are essential in any language. Do you still remember the numbers from one to ten in Chapter 2? Let's cover them again and write them out for practice along with two new words, eleven and twelve, for telling time.

Number	Chinese	
0	líng	_____
1	yī	_____
2	èr	_____
3	sān	_____
4	sì	_____
5	wǔ	_____
6	liù	_____
7	qī	_____
8	bā	_____
9	jiǔ	_____
10	shí	_____
11	shí yī	_____
12	shí èr	_____

Xiànzài Jǐ Diǎn Zhōng?

What Time Is It Now?

Now you're ready to start telling time. Look at the clocks below.

Běijīng
Beijing

Niǔyuē
New York

Bālí
Paris

Ālāsījiā
Alaska

Mòsīkē
Moscow

To tell the time, Chinese use the number plus "**diǎn zhōng**" (o'clock) or without "zhong." For example, one o'clock is **yì diǎn**. Can you count around the clock? Try it just once. To add precision to your time you might want to add the words **zǎoshang** for "in the morning," **xiàwu** for "in the afternoon," or wǎnshang for "in the evening."

Shénme Shíjian

When?

Now that you can tell time, it's easy to tell someone *when* or *at what time* something happened or will happen. You simply put the time before the verb. Study the following examples:

Fēijī	**yì diǎn (zhōng)**	**qǐfēi.**	
(The plane)	(1 o'clock)	(takes off)	
Tā	**sān diǎn (zhōng)**	**lái de.**	
(He)	(3 o'clock)	(came)	
Wǒ	**qī diǎn (zhōng)**	**lái.**	
(I)	(7 o'clock)	(will come)	
Wǒ	**sì diǎn (zhōng)**	**huíjiā.**	
(I)	(4 o'clock)	(come home)	
Tā	**shí diǎn (zhōng)**	**shuìjiào.**	
(She)	(10 o'clock)	(go to bed)	

Now you are ready for some more numbers. Notice that Chinese count their numbers from 11 to 19 by saying **shí** (ten) first and then whatever one-digit number they need. If it is 11, say **shí** (ten) and **yī** (one). Study the following. Try to repeat them aloud and then write them in the blanks provided.

Number	Chinese	
11	**shí yi**	_____
12	**shí èr**	_____
13	**shí sān**	_____
14	**shí sì**	_____
15	**shí wǔ**	_____
16	**shí liù**	_____
17	**shí qī**	_____
18	**shí bā**	_____
19	**shí jiǔ**	_____

32

For the numbers twenty, thirty, forty, fifty, sixty, seventy, eighty, and ninety, you say the one-digit number first and then say *shí* (ten). Take twenty for example. You say **èr** (two) first and then say **shí** (ten).

Number	Chinese	
20	èr shí	_____
30	sān shí	_____
40	sì shí	_____
50	wǔ shí	_____
60	liù shí	_____
70	qī shí	_____
80	bā shí	_____
90	jiǔ shí	_____

To make the numbers twenty-one, twenty-two, etc., just add the single digits from above.

21	22	23
èr shi yī	èr shi èr	èr shi sān

24	25	26
èr shi sì	èr shi wǔ	èr shi liù

27	28	29
èr shi qī	èr shi bā	èr shi jiǔ

Here are some words for larger numbers. Chinese uses **bǎi** for hundred, **qiǎn** for thousand, **wàn** for ten thousand, and **yì** for ten million. Study the following large numbers and be sure to practice them often, until you get the hang of it.

Number	Chinese	
100	yì bǎi	_____
101	yì bǎi líng yī	_____
110	yì bǎi yī shí	_____
200	èr bǎi	_____
300	sān bǎi	_____
400	sì bǎi	_____
500	wǔ bǎi	_____
600	liù bǎi	_____
700	qī bǎi	_____
800	bā bǎi	_____
900	jiǔ bǎi	_____
1000	yì qiān	_____
2000	èr qiān/liǎng qiān	_____
10,000	yí wàn	_____
20,000	èr wàn/liǎng wàn	_____
1,000,000	yì bǎi wàn	_____
100,000,000	yí yì	_____
1,000,000,000	shí yì	_____

Xùshù
Ordinal Numbers

For ordinal numbers, Chinese use **dì** before the number. Write in the floors in the elevator in the spaces provided and say them aloud.

dì jiǔ
ninth

_____

dì qī
seventh

_____

dì wǔ
fifth

_____

dì sān
third

_____

dì yī
first

_____

dì shí
tenth

_____

dì bā
eighth

_____

dì liù
sixth

_____

dì sì
fourth

_____

dì èr
second

_____

More Ways to Tell Time

For plane and train schedules, the 24-hour clock is used, so that the numbers from 13 to 24 designate the P.M. hours.

One o'clock P.M. = **shí sān diǎn**

You may now wonder how to say 1:05 or 1:55, etc. As in English, you say **...diǎn**, the hour first, and then **... fēn**, the minute. For example, 1:05 = **yì diǎn líng wǔ fēn**; 1:55 = **yì diǎn wǔ shí wǔ**.

Can you tell the time? Write your answers in the spaces provided.

a. 1:00 _____

b. 2:05 _____

c. 3:10 _____

d. 4:15 _____

e. 5:20 _____

f. 6:25 _____

g. 7:30 _____

h. 8:35 _____

i. 9:40 _____

j. 10:45 _____

k. 11:50 _____

l. 12:55 _____

In addition to saying twelve o'clock, **shí èr diǎn,** Chinese can say

Noon   **zhōngwǔ**   *or*   Midnight   **wǔyè**

Learn the following important little words by heart to tell time.

diǎn = o'clock

fēn = minute (sometimes omitted)

kè = 15 minutes (a quarter of an hour)

bàn = 30 minutes (a half-hour)

guò = plus, past, after (used before 30 minutes of the hour, sometimes omitted)

chà = minus, to, before (used after 30 minutes of the hour, counting toward the next hour)

Examples:

3:15 **sān diǎn yí kè** (three o'clock plus a quarter)

3:30 **sān diǎn bàn** (three o'clock plus a half)

3:45 **chà yí kè sì diǎn** (four o'clock minus a quarter)

Xiànzài Jǐ Diǎn Le?

What Time Is It?

Tell the time, using **diǎn**, **fēn**, **guò**, **kè**, and **bàn**.

1. _____
It's 12:15.

2. _____
It's 12:45.

3. _____
It's 6:30.

4. _____
It's 7:55.

5. _____
It's 8:05.

6. _____
It's 10:40.

Shǔ Bùtóng Zhǒnglèi De Dōngxī

Counting Different Kinds of Things

We need to count things. In Chinese you need to use special classifiers, or counters (measure words) to go with different kinds of things. Here are some of the most common ones and a few examples to show you how.

one old man	**yí wèi lǎo rén**
one pencil	**yì zhī qiānbǐ**
one book	**yì běn shū**
one ticket	**yì zhāng piào**

people

1. ... **wèi** (with respect)

2. ... **míng** (common word)

things

1. ... **kē** (of plants, trees)

2. ... **běn** (of bound objects e.g. books, notebooks, magazines)

3. ... **zhāng** (of paper, tickets, bills, checks)

4. ... **jià** (of machines, planes, cameras, pianos)

5. ... **dòng** (of buildings, houses)

6. ... **gēn** (long thin objects e.g. chopsticks, hair, pins)

ANSWERS

Tell the time   **1.** Shí èr diǎn (guò) yí kè.   **2.** Chà yí kè yì diǎn.   **3.** Liù diǎn bàn.   **4.** Chà wǔ fēn bā diǎn.   **5.** Bā diǎn líng wǔ fēn.   **6.** Shí diǎn sì shí.

37

7. **... piàn** (of ❶ land, sea ❷ medicine, chips)

8. **... tiáo** (of street, road, path, legs, fish)

9. **... fù** (of a set or a pair of things e.g. glasses, gloves)

10. **... kuài** (of ❶ watches, cakes, bread, soap ❷ money)

11. **... gè** (of almost all other things, including some listed above; It can also be used for people.)

Now back to time! Let's listen to Mark in the following encounter. Look over the text and then repeat the dialogue several times until you are comfortable.

MARK	**Qǐngwèn.**	Excuse me.
	Xiànzài jídiǎn le?	What time is it?
STRANGER	**Shí èr diǎn.**	It's 12 o'clock.
MARK	**Xièxie.**	Thank you.
STRANGER	**Búkèqi.**	You're welcome.
	Nǐde biǎo tíng le ma?	Has your watch stopped working?
MARK	**Méiyǒu.**	Oh, no.
	Wǒde háishì Niǔyuē shíjiān.	It still keeps New York time.
STRANGER	**Nǐ shì yóukè ma?**	Are you a tourist?
MARK	**Duì.**	Yes, I am.
STRANGER	**Yěxǔ nǐ kéyǐ zài zhèr mǎi yī kuài shóubiǎo.**	You might want to buy a watch here.
	Yīlái kéyǐ jì dāngdì shíjiān, yě kéyǐ dàngzuò jìniànpǐn.	It can tell the local time and can be a souvenir.
MARK	**Zhè zhǔyì búcuò.**	A good idea.
	Zhèr yí kuài biǎo duōshǎo qián?	How much does a watch cost here?
STRANGER	**Shóubiǎo zài Zhōngguó bú guì.**	Watches are not expensive in China.

38

Búdào wǔ kuài qián jiù kéyǐ mǎi yī kuài.

You can pick one up for less than five dollars.

MARK **Nà hǎo. Wǒ jiù mǎi yí kuài.**

Good. I'll buy one.

Can you write these phrases from the dialogue in Chinese?

1. Has your watch stopped working? _____

2. My watch still keeps New York time. _____

3. You might want to buy a watch here. _____

4. How much does a watch cost here? _____

5. Watches are not expensive in China. _____

Jīntiān Xīngqī Jǐ?
What Day Is Today?

Chinese name each day of the week by numbers except Sunday. Starting from Monday, they say **xīngqī** (week) +

yī (one)	Monday
èr (two)	Tueday
sān (three)	Wednesday
sì (four)	Thursday
wǔ (five)	Friday
liù (six)	Saturday

For Sunday they say **xīngqī tiān** (day).

jīntiān
today

zuótiān
yesterday

míngtiān
tomorrow

yǐjīng
already

háishì
still

zàicì
again

To say something happened or will happen on a certain day, you simply put the day before the verb as you do with the time.

When do you work?   **Ní nǎ yì tiān gōngzuò?**

I work on Monday.   **Wǒ xīngqī yī gōngzuò.**
    on Tuesday   **xīngqī èr**
    on Wednesday   **xīngqī sǎn**
    on Thursday   **xīngqī sì**
    on Friday   **xīngqī wǔ**

I don't work on Saturday.   **Wǒ xīngqī liù bù gǒngzuò.**
    on Sunday   **xīngqī tiān**

Can you match up the following days of the week and adverbs of time with their English equivalents?

1. xīngqī èr   a. tomorrow

2. xīngqī sān   b. already

3. jīntiān   c. Wednesday

4. yǐjīng   d. yesterday

5. míngtiān   e. again

6. zàicì   f. Tuesday

7. zuótiān   g. today

Hànyǔ Dòngcí
Chinese Verbs

You have already learned that Chinese verbs do not have endings or special forms like English verbs. However, Chinese does use some adverbs around the verb in a sentence to help clarify the time of an action. Here are the three basic ones. Words in parentheses can be omitted.

jiāng (yào) + verb to indicate a future action

(zhèng) zài + verb to indicate an action in progress

verb + **(guò) le** to indicate a past action

Wǒ tiān tiān kàn shū.	I read every day.
Wǒ *jiāng (yào)* **kàn shū.**	I will (am going to) read.
Wǒ *(zhèng) zài* **kàn shū.**	I am reading a book.
Wǒ kàn *(guò) le* **zhè běn shū.**	I (have) read this book.

Now see if you can fill in the blanks.

1. He is working now.　　　　　**Tā** _____.
2. He will work.　　　　　　　**Tā** _____.
3. He worked.　　　　　　　　**Tā** _____.
4. He works every day.　　　　**Tā tiān tiān** _____.

Zài Huǒchē Shàng
On the Train

Lièchē Fúwù
Train Service

Traveling by train can be a pleasant way to travel between cities in China and to catch a glimpse of the countryside and the people. The overnight trains between Beijing and Guangzhou provide a reliable and comfortable opportunity to make acquaintances, avoid weather delays at airports, and get a good night's sleep.

The following dialogue contains important words and phrases connected with train travel. Read it aloud several times.

MARK	**Dào chēzhàn le.**	Here we are at the station.
ANNE	**Bàba, wǒmen shì chéng tèkuài qù Guǎngzhōu ma?**	Dad, are we riding on the express to Guangzhou?
MARK	**Shì.**	Yes. (to the ticket clerk)
	Qù Guǎngzhōu de láihuí chēpiào duōshǎo qián?	How much does a round-trip ticket to Guangzhou cost?
CLERK	**Ruǎnwò háishì yìngwò?**	Soft sleeper or hard sleeper ticket?
MARK	**Qǐng gěi ruǎnwò. Wǒmen yǒu sì gè rén.**	Soft sleeper, please. And there are four of us.
CLERK	**Zǒnggòng sān qiān èr bǎi yuán.**	That will be 3,200 yuan in total.
MARK	**Shénme shíjiān kāichē?**	When does the train depart?

CLERK	Wǎnshang shíyī diǎn sì shi wǔ fēn.	At 11:45 P.M. (23:45).
MARK	Zài nǎ yí ge zhàntái?	From which platform?
CLERK	Zài sì hào zhàntái.	Track #4.
	Zhè shì nǐde chēpiào.	Here are your tickets.
ANNE	Bàba, wǒmende wèizi zài nǎr?	Dad, where are our seats?
MARK	Shí hào chēxiāng, wǔ zhì bā hào zuòwèi.	Car 10, seats 5–8.

Match these Chinese words and expressions with their English equivalents.

1. **huǒchē**   a. platform
2. **chēzhàn**   b. round-trip ticket
3. **láihuí chēpiào** c. train
4. **ruǎnwò**   d. station
5. **zhàntái**   e. soft sleeper
6. **tèkuài**   f. express

Train travel can be an adventure of a lifetime for some Americans. For Chinese people, however, it is an important component of their lifestyle since trains are the major means of long-distance travel in China. So the experience can be worthwhile. Following are some useful words and expressions to deal with rail travel in China.

♦ **tèkuài** (express train) with few stops

♦ **zhíkuài** (fast train) with a few stops

♦ **mànchē** (slow train) with more stops

♦ **ruǎnwò** (soft sleeper) most comfortable, best served, and of course, most expensive

♦ **yìngwò** (hard sleeper) preferred by most long-distance travelers because of its comforts and acceptable price

♦ **ruǎnzuò** (soft seat) very comfortable, and quiet

♦ **yìngzuò** (hard seat) may be very noisy and crowded but a good place to get to know the average Chinese people

Huǒchē
Train

lǚyóu
to travel

chéngkè
passenger

zuòxia
to sit down

zhàn
to stand

hòuchēshì
waiting lounge

zhàntái
platform

jiǎnpiàoyuán
conductor

shíjiānbiǎo
schedule

xínglǐ chē
luggage cart

bānyùngōngrén
porter

Zìjǐ Zuò
Do It Yourself

In English, such words as "myself," "yourself," and "himself" are called reflexive pronouns and emphasizing pronouns. In Chinese, you express the same meaning with the word **zìjǐ**, which means "one's self" and is used for all persons. To form a reflexive or an emphasizing pronoun, simply put **zìjǐ** after the personal pronouns.

myself . . . . wǒ **zìjǐ**

yourself . . . . nǐ **zìjǐ**

himself . . . . tā **zìjǐ**

herself . . . . tā **zìjǐ**

ourselves . . . . wǒmen **zìjǐ**

yourselves . . . . nǐmen **zìjǐ**

themselves . . . . tāmen **zìjǐ**

I hurt myself.   **Wǒ shāngzhe zìjǐ le.**
I am going myself.   **Wǒ zìjǐ qù.**

The following passage is about train travel. Read about Mark and his family. Then answer the questions. (The translation of the passage is given in the answer section.)

Mǎkè hé tā yì jiā yào chéng huǒchē qù Guǎngzhōu. Tāmen zài huǒchēzhàn mǎi le láihuí

chēpiào. Sì zhāng ruǎnwò chēpiào huā le tāmen sān qiān èr bǎi kuài qián.

1. Mǎkè hé tā yì jiā yào chéng huǒchē qù nálǐ?

   _____

2. Tāmen mǎi le shénme chēpiào?

   _____

3. Chēpiào huā le tāmen duōshǎo qián?

   _____

Now let's take a look at the rest of the world and learn how to say the names of the different countries in Chinese. First look at the map and then match the Chinese names with their English counterparts.

Zhōu yǔ Guójiā
Continents and Countries

Africa	**Fēizhōu**	Asia	**Yàzhōu**
America	**Měizhōu**	Australia	**Àozhōu**
North America	**Béi Měizhōu**	Europe	**Ōuzhōu**
South America	**Nán Měizhōu**	Afghanistan	**Āfùhàn**

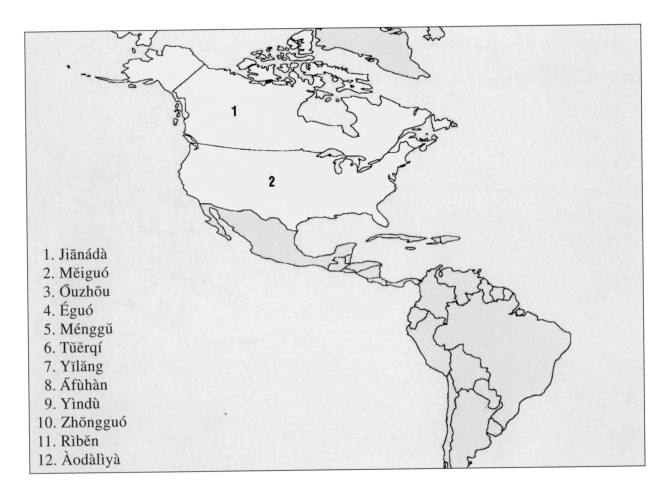

1. Jiānádà
2. Měiguó
3. Ōuzhōu
4. Éguó
5. Ménggǔ
6. Tǔěrqí
7. Yīlǎng
8. Āfùhàn
9. Yìndù
10. Zhōngguó
11. Rìběn
12. Àodàlìyà

Austria	**Àodìlì**	Germany	**Déguó**
Belgium	**Bǐlìshí**	Hungary	**Xiōngyálì**
Brazil	**Bāxī**	India	**Yìndù**
Canada	**Jiānádà**	Iran	**Yīlāng**
China	**Zhōngguó**	Ireland	**Àiěrlán**
England	**Yīngguó**	Israel	**Yǐsèliè**
Estonia	**Àishāníyà**	Italy	**Yìdàlì**
Finland	**Fēnlán**	Japan	**Rìběn**
France	**Fǎguó**	Malaysia	**Mǎláixīyà**
Mongolia	**Ménggǔ**	Spain	**Xībānyá**
Norway	**Nuówēi**	Sweden	**Ruìdiǎn**
Poland	**Bōlán**	Switzerland	**Ruìshì**
Portugal	**Pútáoyá**	Turkey	**Tǔěrqí**
Scotland	**Sūgélán**	United States	**Měiguó**

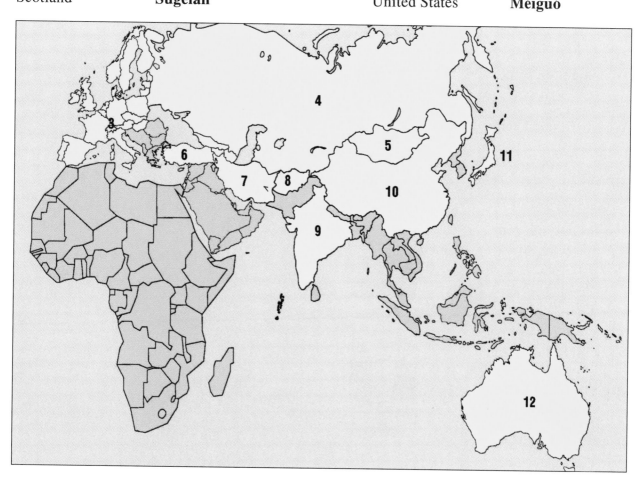

Guójí
Nationalities

It is very easy to tell someone your nationality in Chinese. Simply add **rén** to the name of the country:

Wǒ shì Měiguó rén.   I'm American.

CHINESE		ENGLISH
Wǒ shì Xiōngyálì rén.		I'm Hungarian.
Wǒ shì Àodìlì rén.		I'm Austrian.
Wǒ shì Éguó rén.		I'm Russian.
Wǒ shì Déguó rén.		I'm German.
Wǒ shì Pútáoyá rén.		I'm Portuguese.
Wǒ shì Yìndù rén.		I'm Indian.
Wǒ shì Jiānádà rén.		I'm Canadian.
Wǒ shì Zhōngguó rén.		I'm Chinese.
Wǒ shì Àiěrlán rén.		I'm Irish.
Wǒ shì Yīngguó rén.		I'm British.
Wǒ shì Yǐsèliè rén.		I'm Israeli.
Wǒ shì Yìdàlì rén.		I'm Italian.
Wǒ shì Fēnlán rén.		I'm Finnish.

Wǒ shì Rìběn rén.		I'm Japanese.
Wǒ shì Fǎguó rén.		I'm French.
Wǒ shì Xībānyá rén.		I'm Spanish.
Wǒ shì Nuówēi rén.		I'm Norwegian.
Wǒ shì Bōlán rén.		I'm Polish.
Wǒ shì Tǔěrqí rén.		I'm Turkish.
Wǒ shì Měiguó rén.		I'm American.

Wǒ Diū le Qiánbāo
I've Lost My Purse

Can you imagine how Mary feels when, during a day of shopping and sight-seeing, she discovers she has lost her purse? She approaches a policeman for help.

MARY   **Duìbuqǐ,**   Excuse me,

             nǐ kéyǐ bāng wǒ ma?   can you help me, please?

POLICEMAN	Kéyǐ. Shénme shì?	Yes, what is it?
MARY	Wǒ diū le qiánbāo.	I've lost my purse.
POLICEMAN	Nǐde qiánbāo?	Your purse?
	Zài nǎr diū de?	Where did you lose it?
MARY	Wǒ bù zhīdao.	I don't know.
	Wǒ gāng xià dìtiě.	I just got off the subway.
	Wǒ gāi zěnme bàn?	What should I do?
POLICEMAN	Yǒu yǒujiàzhí de dōngxī ma?	Any valuables?
MARY	Yǒu. Wǒde hùzhào, xìnyòng kǎ, hé lǚxíng zhīpiào.	Yes. My passport, credit cards, and travelers' checks.
POLICEMAN	Qù wènwen shīwùzhāolǐng chù. Rénmen tōngcháng bǎ shí dào de dōngxi jiāo dào nàlǐ.	Check with the Lost and Found Office. People usually turn in the lost items there.
MARY	Xièxie nǐde jiànyì.	Thanks for the advice.
	Shīwùzhāolǐng chù zài nǎr?	Where is that office?
POLICEMAN	Zhè tiáo jiē jiù yǒu yí gè.	There is one right on this street.
MARY	Nà tài hǎo le.	Good.

Driving in China is another adventure and is not for the fainthearted! Although most of the traffic regulations are pretty much the same as those in the United States, most expressway signs are in Chinese. Non-express roads may be narrow and usually are crowded with pedestrians, bicycles, city buses, and cars.

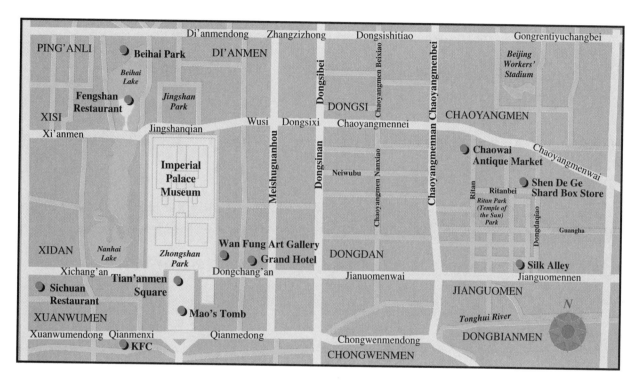

Zūchē
Renting a Car

Mark is a brave, adventurous soul. He has decided to rent a car and take his family for a ride to see more of the countryside. He is now at the car rental office.

MARK	**Zǎoshàng hǎo. Wǒ xiǎng zū yí liàng chē.**	Good morning. I would like to rent a car.
WOMAN	**Nàhǎo. Zū duō cháng shíjiān?**	Certainly. For how long?
MARK	**Dàyuē yì xīngqī.**	About a week.
WOMAN	**Nǐ xiǎng yào duōdà de chē?**	What size car do you prefer?
MARK	**Nǐmen yǒu xiǎo miànbāochē ma?**	Do you have a minivan?

WOMAN	Wǒmen yǒu.	Yes, we do.
	Zhè shì xiǎo miànbāochē de jiàgé.	Here is the price for minivans.
MARK	Zhè jiàgé bāokuò lǐchéng ma?	Is the mileage included in the price?
WOMAN	Bāokuò. Nǐ zìjǐ fù yóu fèi.	Yes, but you pay for the gas.
	Qǐng bǎ nǐde jiàzhào hé	May I have your driver's license
	xìnyòng kǎ gěi wǒ.	and credit card, please?
MARK	Hǎo de. Zài zhèr.	Sure. Here they are.
WOMAN	Qǐng zài zhèr qiānzì.	Please sign here.
MARK	Hǎode.	OK.
WOMAN	Xièxie. Zhù nǐ lǚtú yúkuài.	Thank you. Have a good trip!

Now let's see if you can rent a car, using your Chinese. Fill in the blanks below with the correct words or expressions. The English meaning is given in the brackets.

1. Wǒ _____ yí liàng chē. (would like to rent)

2. Zhè jiàgé _____ ma? (include mileage)

3. Nǐmen _____ ma? (have a minivan)

4. Qǐng _____. (Sign here)

5. Nǐ zìjǐ _____. (pay for the gas)

Lù Biāo
Road Signs

If you're planning to drive while you're abroad, it's important to spend some time memorizing the meanings of these signs.

Fúwùqū
Service Area

Wēixiǎn
Danger

Tíng
Stop

Jǐnjí diànhuà
Emergency Telephone

Xiàn sù
Speed Limit

Jiěchú xiàn sù
End of Speed Limit

Jìnzhǐ shǐrù
No Entrance

Ràng
Yield Right of Way

Jìnzhǐ zuǒzhuǎn
No Left Turn

Gāosù gōnglù
Expressway

Gāosù gōnglù zhōngdiǎn
End of Expressway

Yìhuá
Slippery

Jìnzhǐ chāochē
No Passing

Jiěchú jìnzhǐ chāochē
End of No Passing Zone

Dānxiàng xíngshǐ
One-way Traffic

Shuāngxiàng xíngshǐ
Two-way Traffic

Zuǒdào zhōngzhǐ
Left Lane Ends

Tíngchēchǎng
Parking

Jìnzhǐ mínglǎbā
No Horn

Huándào xíngshǐ
Roundabout

Jìnzhǐ diàotóu
No U-turn

Jìnzhǐ tíngchē
No Parking

Shízìlùkǒu
Intersection

Rénxíng héngdào
Pedestrian Crossing

Tiělùdàokǒu
Railroad Crossing

Suìdào
Tunnel

Zài Jiāyóuzhàn

At the Service Station

MARK	Qǐng bāng wǒ jiāmǎn, hǎoma?	Could you fill it up, please?
CASHIER	Yìbān de háishì chāojí de?	Regular or super?
MARK	Qǐng gěi chāojí de. Qǐng nǐ bāng wǒ jiǎnchá yíxià jīyóu, shuǐ, hé lúntāi, hǎoma?	Super, please. Could you check the oil, water, and tires, please?
CASHIER	Měi yíyàng dōu hěn hǎo.	Everything's OK.
MARK	Wǒmen xiǎng qù dòngwùyuán. Wǒmen zěnme zǒu?	We want to go to the zoo. How can we get there?
CASHIER	Yìzhí zǒu dàyuē shí gōnglǐ, ránhòu, yòu guǎi.	Straight ahead about 10 kilometers, and then to the right.
MARK	Xièxie. Zàijiàn.	Thank you. Good-bye.

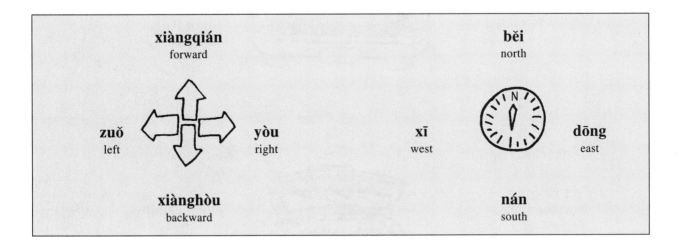

Qìchē
Car

lǎba
horn

fāngxiàngpán
steering wheel

líhéqì tàbǎn
clutch pedal

shāchē tàbǎn
brake pedal

yǔshuā
windshield wiper

yíbiǎopán
instrument panel (dashboard)

biànsù gǎn
gear shift stick

yóumén
accelerator

dǎngfēng bōli
windshield

mǎdá
motor

shuǐxiāng
radiator

chēgài
hood

diànpíng
battery

qiándēng
headlights

dàochēdēng
backup light

fāngxiàngdēng
turn signal

shāchēdēng
brake light

hòuchēxiāng
trunk

hòuchēchuāng
rear window

wěidēng
rear light

chēpáizhào
license plate

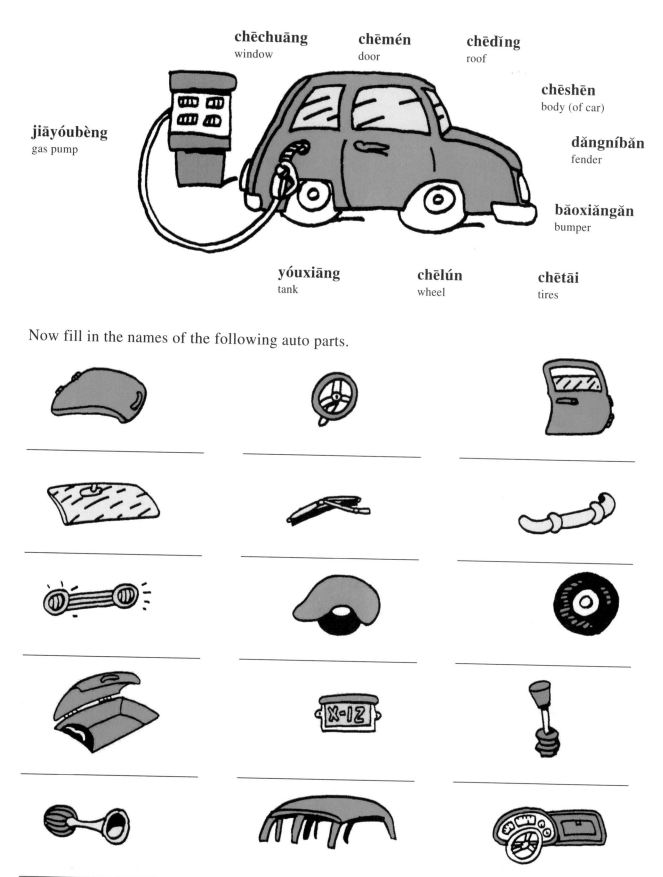

chēchuāng
window

chēmén
door

chēdǐng
roof

chēshēn
body (of car)

jiāyóubèng
gas pump

dǎngníbǎn
fender

bǎoxiǎngǎn
bumper

yóuxiāng
tank

chēlún
wheel

chētāi
tires

Now fill in the names of the following auto parts.

57

Qiúyuán

Help!

Here are some useful phrases in case of problems with your car:

Wǒde chētāi méi qì le.	I have a flat tire.
Chē fādòng bù liǎo le.	The car won't start.
Wǒde chē huài le.	My car has broken down.
Chē guòrè le.	It's overheating.
Wǒde chē méi yóu le.	I've run out of gas.
Shuǐxiāng lòushuǐ.	The radiator is leaking.
Diànpíng yòngwán le.	The battery is dead.
Qǐng jiǎnchá yíxià	Please check the
diànpíng.	battery.
shāchē	brakes
xiāoyīnqì	muffler
jīyóu	oil
chētāi	tires

Qíshǐ Yǔqì

Imperative Mood

You've already learned several ways to ask for things in Chinese. Now let's look at another way, the imperative, or command form of the verb.

An imperative sentence in Chinese is a request or command made to the listener, usually the second person "you." As the subject is clear and understood, it is omitted from the sentence.

(Nǐ) Zuòxià.   (You) sit down.

Qǐng (please) may be used before the verb to show politeness. In this case, keeping the subject in the sentence sounds more polite.

Qǐng zuòxià.   Please sit down.
Qǐng nín zuòxià.   Would you please sit down?

Búyào, Bié, or Jìnzhǐ (don't, do not, no) is used before the verbs to form a negative imperative sentence. Jìnzhǐ is a word expressing prohibition and is used in writing only.

Búyào zuòxià.	Don't sit down.
Bié zuòxià.	Don't sit down.
Jìnzhǐ xīyān!	No smoking!

If the subject is "I" or "We," Chinese use the word **Ràng** before the subject. It is like the English "Let me..." or "Let's...."

Ràng wǒ dǎkāi chuānghu.	Let me open the window.
Ràng wǒmen qù sànbù.	Let's go for a walk.

Sometimes you don't want to sound too "bossy." You can use the word **ba** at the end of the sentence to soften your tone.

Zuòxià ba.	Sit down, please.
Búyào zài zhèr xīyān ba!	Please don't smoke here, will you?

Try to make the following imperative sentences sound more polite. Write your answers in the spaces provided.

1. **Bāngzhù wǒ.** (Help me!) _____

2. **Jiǎnchá yíxià jīyóu.** (Check the oil.) _____

3. **Kàn zhèr.** (Look here.) _____

4. **Jìnlai.** (Come in.) _____

Try to change these sentences into negative forms. Write your answers in the spaces provided.

5. **Bāngzhù wǒ.** (Help me!) _____

6. **Jiǎnchá jīyóu.** (Check the oil.) _____

7. **Kàn zhèr.** (Look here.) _____

8. **Jìnlai.** (Come in.) _____

Qíyuàn Yǔqì

Optative Verbs

Néng, Kéyǐ, Huì, Xiǎng, and **Yuànyì** are the basic words (optative verbs) that are used before the predicate verbs (or adjectives) to indicate ability, willingness, desire, and so forth.

Néng means ability to do something or permission to do certain things.

Wǒ míngtiān néng zǎo lái wǔ fēn zhōng.
I can come five minutes earlier tomorrow.

Wǒmen xiàbān hòu yǒu ge huìyì. Wǒ bù néng wǔ diǎn huíjiā.
We have a meeting after work. I can't go home at 5 o'clock.

Kéyǐ functions and means the same as **Néng** in an affirmative sentence. In the negative form **bù kéyǐ** implies prohibition.

Wǒ kéyǐ xiān dásǎo fángjiān.
I can clean the room first.

A: **Wǒmen kéyǐ zài zhèr zhàoxiàng ma?**   B: **Bù kéyǐ.**
A: May we take pictures here?   B: No, you mustn't.

Huì implies subjective ability acquired through learning.

Wǒ huì shuō Hànyǔ.   I can speak Chinese.

Xiǎng means intention or desire to do something.

Wǒ xiǎng zū yí liàng chē.
I want to rent a car.

Yuànyì means willingness.

Wǒ yuànyì bāngzhù tāmen.
I am willing to help them.

Now let's try to use these optative verbs in the following mini-dialogue. Fill in the blanks with **néng**, **kéyǐ**, **huì**, **xiǎng**, or **yuànyì**.

Dialogue # 1

A: **Nǐ _____ qí zìxíngchē ma?**
    (1)

A: Can you ride a bike?

B: **Wǒ bú _____ .**
        (2)

B: I can't.

A: **Wǒ _____ jiāo nǐ.**
        (3)

A: I am willing to help you.

B: **Zhèr _____ xué qí zìxíngchē ma?**
        (4)

B: Can we learn to ride a bike here?

A: **_____ .**
    (5)

A: Sure.

Dialogue # 2

A: **Mǎkè _____ qù Chángchéng.**
        (6)

A: Mark wants to go to the Great Wall.

B: **Tā _____ zìjǐ qù ma?**
        (7)

B: Can he go by himself?

A: **Wǒ bù zhīdao.**
    Nǐ _____ dài tā qù ma?
        (8)

A: I don't know.
    Would you like to take him there?

B: **_____ .**
        (9)

B: Yes, I'd love to.

ANSWERS

Dialogue #1 (1) huì (2) huì (3) yuànyì (4) kéyǐ (5) Kéyǐ
Dialogue #2 (6) xiǎng (7) néng (8) yuànyì (9) Yuànyì

61

Wǒmen Xūyào de Měiyíyàng Dōngxī
Everything That We Need

zhàngpeng
tent

yīfu
clothes

shù
tree

tàiyáng
sun

shuìdài
sleeping bag

shǒudiàntǒng
flashlight

xióng
bear

dúmùzhōu
canoe

tǎnzi
blanket

shǒuzhǐ
toilet paper

lánzi
basket

guàntou
cans

píxuē
boots

diàoyúgān
fishing rod

kāisāizuàn
corkscrew

guō
pots

tǒng
bucket

shùxǐ yòngjù
toilet kit

shōuyīnjī
radio

huǒchái
matches

That's a lot of new words and expressions to remember! Let's play a little game. Look at the word maze below and see how many words associated with camping you can identify. Circle the words and then write them out in the spaces below. We have already found the first word for you.

N	P	I	A	D	I	U	H	S	Z	E	F	I
D	D	T	O	N	G	F	M	H	T	D	J	C
O	I	Q	O	L	F	H	A	G	L	I	T	I
Q	A	J	A	S	A	N	E	S	C	A	H	J
S	N	S	T	U	G	N	T	F	O	O	N	F
C	T	I	H	P	D	O	Z	O	T	Y	V	E
Y	O	D	E	O	T	I	L	I	E	U	O	T
I	N	N	A	U	A	A	E	W	G	Q	P	
V	G	V	N	D	A	Y	Z	H	O	A	X	H
U	N	Z	F	A	T	F	I	K	C	N	V	L
F	I	O	A	D	N	O	O	N	G	O	D	G
I	G	U	A	N	T	O	U	N	J	T	U	D
N	U	D	A	G	S	C	A	T	C	I	K	H

_____   _____

_____   _____

_____   _____

_____   _____

_____   _____

Lùyíng

Camping

Mark and Mary have already rented a car and are about to set off on their own. Let's see how they make out.

MARK — **Qǐngwèn, zhè fùjìn yǒu lùyíngdì ma?** — Excuse me. Is there a campsite nearby?

FARMER — **Yǒu. Lí zhèr dàyuē èr shí gōnglǐ. Nàr huì yǒu yí gè páizi.** — Yes. About 20 kilometers from here. There will be a sign.

MARK — **Nàr yǒu guànxǐshì hé yǐnyòng shuǐ ma?** — Are there any bathrooms there? And drinking water?

FARMER — **Kěndìng yǒu.** — I'm sure there are.

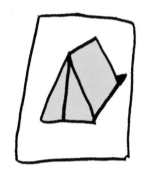

Zài Fùshí Diàn

At the Grocery Store

MARK — **Zǎoshàng hǎo. Wǒ yào yì gōngjīn mǐ, bàn gōngjīn huǒtuǐ, hé yì tiáo miànbāo.** — Good morning. I need a kilo of rice, a half kilo of ham, and a loaf of bread.

CLERK — **Hái yào biéde dōngxi ma? Yào diǎn jiǔ huò ruǎnyǐnliào ma?** — Anything else? Any wine or soft drinks?

MARK	**Bú yào le. Xièxie. Jiù zhèxiē.**	No, thank you. That's all.
	Wǒ yào fù duōshǎo qián?	How much do I owe you?
CLERK	**Wǔ shí kuài.**	50 yuan.
MARK	**Gěi nǐ qián.**	Here you are.
	Zàijiàn.	Good-bye.

Let's see if you remember the useful words and phrases from the preceding dialogues, which might come in handy.

1. _____

   Is there a campsite nearby?

2. _____

   There will be a sign.

3. _____

   drinking water

4. _____

   Any wine or soft drinks?

5. _____

   How much do I owe you?

More About Verbs

Now you know when the particle **le** is placed after a verb it shows that the action is completed. This can refer to a past action or a future action.

Wǒ chī le zǎofàn.
I have eaten my breakfast.

Míngtiān wǒ chī le zǎofàn, jiù qù gōngyuán.
I will go to the park after I finish eating my breakfast.

ANSWERS

1. Zhè fùjìn yǒu lùyíngdì ma? 2. Nàr huì yǒu yí ge páizi. 3. yǐnyòng shuǐ 4. Yào diǎn jiǔ huò ruǎnyǐnliào ma? 5. Wǒ yào fù duōshǎo qián?

65

In the negative form, sentences of this kind have the particle **le** dropped and the adverb **méi (yǒu)** inserted before the main verb.

Wǒ méi (yǒu) chī zǎofàn.
I have not yet had my breakfast.

Yǒu in the **méi (yǒu)** is often omitted. But it cannot be omitted at the end of a sentence. Together they form a question. The particle **le** is also put after the verb in the sentence.

Nǐ chī le zǎofàn méi yǒu?
Have you had your breakfast?

Wǒmen dào le méi yǒu?
Have we arrived yet?

Wǒmen dào le.
We have arrived.

Wǒmen méi (yǒu) dào.
We have not yet arrived.

Now match the following Chinese expressions with their English equivalents

1. **Tā mǎi le yì běn shū.**
2. **Tā méi (yǒu) mǎi yì běn shū.**
3. **Tā mǎi le yì běn shū méi yǒu?**

a. Has he bought a book?

b. He bought a book.

c. He has not bought a book.

10 Jìjié Yuèfèn

Jìjié
Seasons of the Year

Yuèfèn
Months

Tiānqì
Weather

Xīngqī
Days of the Week

dōng jì
winter

shí èr yuè

yī yuè

èr yuè

chūn jì
spring

sān yuè

sì yuè

wǔ yuè

xià jì
summer

liù yuè

qī yuè

bā yuè

qiū jì
fall

jǐu yuè

shí yuè

shí yī yuè

Yuèfèn

The Months

Please notice that Chinese number the months from January to December with one to twelve. They say the number plus the word **yuè** (month) to indicate a particular month. For example, say **yī** (one), and then **yuè** (month), and you get January.

yī yuè
January

sì yuè
April

qī yuè
July

shí yuè
October

èr yuè
February

wǔ yuè
May

bā yuè
August

shí yī yuè
November

sān yuè
March

liù yuè
June

jiǔ yuè
September

shí èr yuè
December

Tiānqì

The Weather

Jīntiān tiānqì zěnyàng?

How is the weather today?

Jīntiān Tiānqì _____ .

The weather today is _____ .

hǎo
good

huài
bad

Jīntiān tiānqì zhēn hǎo!

What splendid weather!

Jīntiān (hěn) _____ .

Today it's _____ .

nuǎnhuo
warm

rè
hot

liángshuǎng
cool

lěng
cold

Qíngtiān.
It's sunny.

Zài guāfēng.
It is windy.

Zài xiàyǔ.
It's raining.

Zài xiàxuě.
It's snowing.

Can you describe the weather in the pictures below?

1. _____

3. _____

2. _____

4. _____

Chinese use the Celsius scale to measure temperature. It is represented by the symbol C. Water freezes at 0 degree and boils at 100 degrees.

Temperature Conversions

To change degrees Fahrenheit to Celsius subtract 32 and multiply by $5/9$:

$$41°F - 32 = 9 \times 5/9 = 5°C$$

To convert from Celsius to Fahrenheit, multiply by $9/5$ and add 32:

$$10°C \times 9/5 = 18 + 32 = 50°F$$

A quick method to get an approximate temperature is to take the degrees Fahrenheit, subtract 30 and divide by 2. From Celsius, multiply by 2 and add 30.

Most seasoned travelers know a few temperatures for reference.

Dùshu
Degrees

Huáshì Fahrenheit		**Shèshì** Celsius
212		100
98.6		37
86		30
77		25
68		20
50		10
32		0
14		– 10
– 04		– 20
– 22		– 30
– 40		– 40

Wēndùjì
Thermometer

It should be a small consolation that at minus 40, degrees Fahrenheit and Celsius are identical.

Wǒ hěn lěng.
I am cold.

Wǒ hěn rè.
I am hot.

Xīngqī

Days of the Week

Do you remember the days of the week in Chinese? If not, here's a brief review.

xīngqī yī	**xīngqī èr**	**xīngqī sān**	**xīngqī sì**
Monday	Tuesday	Wednesday	Thursday

xīngqī wǔ	**xīngqī liù**	**xīngqī tiān**
Friday	Saturday	Sunday

For days of the month, Chinese first say the month and then use numbers plus the word **hào**.

Examples:
March 3 → **sān yuè sān hào**
April 4 → **sì yuè sì hào**
May 5 → **wǔ yuè wǔ hào**

Do you think you can say and write the days of the month?

1. January 10 _____
2. March 9 _____
3. May 6 _____
4. July 21 _____
5. September 19 _____
6. November 8 _____

7. February 5 _____
8. April 2 _____
9. June 3 _____
10. August 31 _____
11. October 4 _____
12. December 30 _____

ANSWERS

1. yī yuè shí hào
2. sān yuè jiǔ hào
3. wǔ yuè liù hào
4. qī yuè èrshíyī hào
5. jiǔ yuè shí jiǔ hào
6. shí yī yuè bā hào

7. èr yuè wǔ hào
8. sì yuè èr hào
9. liù yuè sān hào
10. bā yuè sānshíyī hào
11. shí yuè sì hào
12. shí èr yuè sānshí hào

71

Xíngróngcí
Adjectives

Unlike English, the Chinese adjective can be used as a predicate in a sentence. In this case, **hěn** is often used before the adjectives, like the English verb "to be." But **hěn** is not a verb. It is an adverb, meaning "very, quite, or rather."

In English we say	The house is big.
In Chinese you say	**Zhè fángzi hěn dà.**

Without **hěn,** comparison or contrast is often implied.

Zhè suǒ fángzi dà. Nà suǒ fángzi xiǎo.
This house is big. That one is small.

However, in answering an alternative question, **hěn** may be left out.

Nǐmende fángzi dà bu dà?	Is your house big or not?
Wǒmende fángzi hěn dà.	Our house is big.

To make a negative form, simply add **bù** before the adjectives.

Zhè suǒ fángzi bú dà.   This house is not big.

Like the English adjectives, the Chinese ones are also used as attributives.

If one character (or a word of a single syllable) is used as an attributive, it goes right before the noun.

xīn shǔ	a new book
dà fángjiān	a big room

If more characters are used as an attributive, the structural particle **de** is usually required. adj. (of more than one syllables) + **de** + noun

hěn dà de fángjiān	a very big room
gānjìng de fángjiān	a clean room

Fēijīchǎng
Airport

When you find the following useful words in the picture, write them out in the spaces provided.

jiǎnpiào _____
check in (registration)

bānjī _____
airliner

xínglǐ _____
luggage

zhōng _____
clock

hǎiguān guānyuán _____
customs officer

hǎiguān _____
customs

fēixíngyuán _____
pilot

kōngzhōng xiǎojiě _____
stewardess

zìdòng lóutī _____
escalator

chūkǒu _____
exit

Fēijī
Airplane

Pronounce aloud the following items connected with airline flight as you search for some of them in the picture above. If you wish, you can write them out for practice.

zuòwèi
seat

_____

dēngjī
boarding

_____

jǐnjí chūkǒu
emergency exit

_____

fēijīzuòcāng
cabin

_____

jiàshǐcāng
cockpit

_____

qǐfēi
takeoff

_____

ānquándài
seat belt

_____

pái
row

_____

hángbān
flight

_____

chéngkè
passenger

_____

jīzǔ rényuán
crew

_____

tuōpán
tray

_____

pǎodào
runway

_____

zhuólù
landing

_____

Mark and his family are on their way back to Beijing and have decided to fly instead of taking the train.

STEWARDESS	**Qǐng chūshì nínde dēngjīpái.**	Your boarding pass, please.
MARK	**Zài zhèr.**	Here they are.
STEWARDESS	**Nǐmende zuòwèi jiù zài nàbiān.**	Your seats are right over there.
MARK	**Xièxie.**	Thank you.
STEWARDESS	**Huānyíng chéngzuò Nánfāng Hángkōng Gōngsī qī shí hào hángbān. Wǒmen hěn kuài jiùyào qǐfēi le. Qǐng jì hǎo ānquándài,zūnshǒu jìnzhǐ xīyān xìnhào.**	We welcome you on board South Airline Flight 70. We will take off in a few minutes. Please fasten your seat belts and observe the no smoking sign.
PILOT	**Zǎoshàng hǎo. Běncì hángbān fēiwǎng Běijīng xūyào sān gè xiǎo shí. Wǒmende gāodù shì yī wàn gōngchǐ. Sùdù wéi měi xiǎo shí qī bǎi wǔ shí gōnglǐ.**	Good morning. Our flight to Beijing takes 3 hours. Our altitude is 10,000 meters. The speed is 750 km per hour.
MARK	**Qǐngwèn, xiǎojiě. Nǐmen gōngyìng fànshí ma?**	Excuse me, miss. Do you serve meals on this flight?

STEWARDESS	**Wǒmen bù gōngyìng. Búguò wǒmen mǎshàng gōngyìng ruǎnyǐnliào hé diǎnxīn.**	No, we don't. But we'll serve some soft drinks and a snack soon.
MARK	**Zhīdao le.**	I see.
PAUL	**Qǐng gěi wǒ yí ge zhěntou hé tǎnzi, hǎo ma?**	May I have a pillow and blanket, please?

STEWARDESS	Hǎo. Gěi nǐ.		Sure. Here you are.
PILOT	Gèwèi chéngkè, jǐ fēn zhōng hòu wǒmen jiùyào zhuólù dào Běijīng le. Wàimiàn zài xiàyǔ. Wēndù shì shèshì èr shí wǔ dù.		Dear passengers, in a few minutes we will be landing in Beijing. It's raining outside. The temperature is 25°C.

Try matching the important phrases in column one with those in column two. Write out the Chinese for practice.

1. Jìnzhǐ xīyān.

    a. Do you serve meals on this flight?

_____

2. Nǐmen gōngyìng fànshí ma?

    b. It's raining outside.

_____

3. Qǐng chūshì nínde dēngjīpái.

    c. No smoking.

_____

4. Qǐng jì hǎo ānquándài.

    d. Please fasten your seat belts.

_____

5. Wàimiàn zài xiàyǔ.

    e. The temperature is 25°C.

_____

6. Wēndù shì shèshì èr shī wǔ dù.

    f. We will soon be landing in Beijing.

_____

7. Wǒmen hěn kuài jiùyào qǐfēi le.

    g. We will take off in a few minutes.

_____

8. Wǒmen jiùyào zhuólù dào Běijīng le.

    h. Your boarding pass, please.

_____

Jiānglái
Future Time

When you want to say that something is going to take place immediately, simply put your verb into the following pattern: **"yào . . . le"**:

> **Dōngtiān (jiù)yào dào le.**   Winter is coming soon.

Yào may be preceded by **jiù** or **kuài** to show urgency.

> **Wǒmen hěn kuài (jiù)yào qǐfēi le.**   We will take off in a few minutes.

When you know what time something will happen, use only **jiùyào** before your verb.

> **Huǒchē sān diǎn jiùyào kāichē le.**   The train will leave at 3 o'clock.

Complete the sentences with **"yào . . . le"**:

1. **Fēijī _____ qǐfēi _____ .**   The plane will take off.
    (plane)   (take off)

2. **Dōngtiān _____ guòqù _____ .**   The winter will soon be over.
    (winter)   (be over)

3. **Tā _____ dào jiā _____ .**   He will be home in a few minutes.
    (He)   (get home)

Zài Chénglǐ
In the City

Back in Beijing, Mark decides to do some sight-seeing.

MARK   **Qǐngwèn, Xiānsheng. Nǐ néng gàosu wǒ Yíhéyuán zài nǎr ma?**   Excuse me, sir, can you tell me where the Summer Palace is?

PASSERBY	Kéyǐ. Wǒ yě qù nèige fāngxiàng. Wǒ huì gàosu nǐ de.	Yes, I'm also going in that direction. I'll show you.
MARK	Nà tàihǎo le.	That's great.
PASSERBY	Nǐ qùguò qítā fēngjǐng diǎn ma?	Have you been to other scenic spots?
MARK	Qùguò. Zuótiān wǒmen qù le Tiānānmén Guǎngchǎng, kàn le Qiánmén, Rénmíndàhuìtáng, hé lìshǐ bówùguǎn. Wǒmen hái qù le Gùgōng.	Yes. Yesterday we went to Tiananmen Square. We saw Qianmen, the Great Hall of the People, and the Museum of History. We also went to the Imperial Palace.
PASSERBY	Nǐmen qùguò Chángchéng le ma?	Have you been to the Great Wall?
MARK	Hái méi yǒu ne.	Not yet.
PASSERBY	Nǐmen yīnggāi qù.	You should go.
MARK	Wǒmen dǎsuàn míngtiān qù.	We are planning to go there tomorrow.
PASSERBY	Chéngchē dàyuē xūyào liǎng xiǎoshí. Nǐmen zhènghǎo yǒu jīhuì kàn kan xiāngcūn. Nǐmen kéyǐ shùndào tíngxià cānguān Shísān Líng.	It takes about two hours by bus to get there. That gives you a chance to see some of the countryside. You can stop to visit the Ming Tombs on your way.
MARK	Nà hěn búcuò.	That sounds good.

ENTERTAINMENT

Yúlè

| 12 | **Xìjù**
Theater | **Diànyǐng**
Movies | **Jiérì**
Holidays |

Xìjù
Theater

No trip to China is complete without a generous sampling of theater, music, and movies. For most Chinese, plays are second in popularity to their beloved opera. Traditional Chinese opera has a history of more than 800 years. It is an art form that integrates singing, music, dialogue, dance, and acrobatics. There are more than 300 different operatic forms in China. The best known is Beijing Opera (**Jīngxì**), which originated in Anhui over 200 years ago. In acting and acrobatic fighting, different roles follow different patterns, and their movements and gestures are stylized, suggestive, and symbolic. The fans enjoy the acting as much as the singing.

Mark and Mary want to go and experience for themselves the authentic arts of China. They are trying to decide what to see and where to go.

MARY	**Jīntiān wǎnshàng nǐ xiǎng qù kàn xì ma?**	Do you want to go to the theater this evening?
MARK	**Hǎo zhǔyì.**	A good idea!
MARY	**Zài Shǒudū Jùyuàn yǒu yìchǎng huàjù Běijīng Rén.**	In the Capital Theater there's the play *Beijing Man.*
	Zài Rénmín Jùyuàn yǒu yìchǎng Jīngxì.	In the People's Theater there's a Beijing opera.
MARK	**Wǒ yìzhí dōu xiǎng kàn yìchǎng Jīngxì.**	I have always wanted to see a Beijing opera.
MARY	**Kěshì yào yǎn sān xiǎoshí.**	But it's three hours long.
	Nǐ zhēnde xiǎng kàn ma?	Do you really like that?

MARK	**Shìde.**	Yes.
	Wǒ xiǎng qù jīnglì yíxià.	I want to experience it.
MARY	**Wǒ lái dǎ diànhuà kàn**	I'll call to see
	yǒu méi yǒu piào.	if there are tickets available.
MARK	**Rúguǒ yǒu piào,**	If there are tickets available,
	jiù dìng liǎng zhāng lóutīng	order two in the balcony,
	de, hǎo ma?	will you?
MARY	**Wǒ shìshi.**	I'll try.

Try to learn the following words. Read them aloud and practice writing them in the spaces provided.

xìjù  theater

lóutīng  balcony

_____

_____

xǐjù  comedy

bēijù  tragedy

_____

_____

zhǔyì idea

bāléi ballet

_____

_____

gējù   opera

gēqǔ   melody

Diànyǐng
Movies

Mary and Mark are discussing what movie they want to see.

MARY **Wǒmen jīnwǎn qù kàn diànyǐng ba.**
Let's go to the movies tonight.

MARK **Lí zhèr bù yuǎn de yìjiā diànyǐngyuàn zài fàngyìng yí bù xiàndài Zhōngguó yǐngpiān.**
In the movie theater not far from here a contemporary Chinese film is playing.

MARY **Yǐngpiān yǒu zìmù ma?**
A film with subtitles?

MARK **Méi yǒu. Méi yǒu zìmù.**
No. Without subtitles.

MARY **Nà wǒmen zěnme kàndedǒng? Wǒ zhīdao nǐ yòu shì xiǎng tǐyàn tǐyàn.**
Then how can we understand it? I know, you just want to experience it again.

(At the ticket office)

MARK	**Liǎng zhāng wǎnshang de piào.**	Two tickets for the evening show.
CLERK	**Yào jìnyìdiǎn de háishì yuǎnyìdiǎn de?**	Do you like ones closer or further away (from the screen)?
MARK	**Búyào tàijìn de.**	Not too close.
MARY	**Diànyǐngpiào búsuàn hěn guì.**	The tickets are not so expensive.
MARK	**Kěbú, zhè shì zài Zhōngguó.**	Well, this is China.

About the Word Yī

1. Pronunciation

Yī is pronounced in the first tone when it stands alone, or at the end of a phrase, or in a telephone number. It is pronounced in the fourth tone (**yì**), when it precedes a syllable of the first, second, and third tone.

yì zhāng piào	one ticket
yì tiáo lù	a road
yì běn shū	a book

Yī is pronounced in the second tone (**Yí**), when it is followed by a fourth tone.

yí kuài qián	one dollar
yí liàng qìchē	a car

2. The omission of **yī**

When **yī** is used before a measure word and not at the beginning of a sentence, **yī** is often omitted in spoken Chinese.

A. I have a book.   **Wǒ you yì běn shū.**   or   **Wǒ yǒu běn shū.**

B. A car is very expensive here.   **Yí liàng qìchē zài zhèr hěn guì.**

82

Jiérì
Holidays

China has only four official public holidays, which are listed below. On these holidays schools and offices are closed. Families gather together.

yíyuè 1 rì	**Yuándàn**	January 1—New Year's Day
wǔyuè 1 rì	**Láodòngjié**	May 1—Worker's Day
shíyuè 1 rì	**Guóqìngjié**	October 1—National Day
yíyuè huò èryuè	**Chūnjié**	January or February (according to cycles in the Chinese lunar calendar)—Chinese New Year

There are some holidays that are traditionally observed in China.

Zhōngqiūjié	Mid-fall Festival
Duānwǔjié	Dragon Boat Festival
Qīngmíngjié	Clear and Bright (April 4, 5, or 6)

Practice saying the following sentences. They might be helpful at the right occasions.

Shēngrì kuàilè!	Happy Birthday!
Jiérì yúkuài!	Happy Holiday!
Xīnnián kuàilè!	Happy New Year!

Mark meets a college student at a coffee shop. The young man is explaining to Mark the Chinese holidays. Let's listen to their conversation.

MARK **Nǐmen dōu yǒu nǎxiē jiérì?** — What holidays do you have?

STUDENT **Wǒmen yǒu sìge zhèngshìde jiérì. Yíyuè 1 rì, wǒmen guò Yuándàn. Láodòngjié zài wǔyuè yí rì. Shíyuè yí rì shì Guóqìngjié. Chūnjié shì zuì zhòngyàode jiérì.** — We have four official holidays. On January 1st, we have New Year's Day. May Day is on May 1. October 1 is our National Day. Spring Festival is the most important holiday.

MARK	Rénmen zài zhèxiē jiérì gàn shénme?	What do people do on these holidays?
STUDENT	Duōshù jiātíng tuánjù zài yìqǐ. Yǒuxiē rén guàng shāngdiàn huò bàifāng qīnyǒu. Yǒuxiē kěnéng qù jiāoyóu huò cóngshì qítāde yúlè huódòng.	Most people have family reunions. Some people go shopping, or visit relatives and friends. Some may go on an outing or do some recreational activities.
MARK	Shèngdànjié zài wǒguó shì ge hěn zhòngyàode jiérì. Nǐmen guò Shèngdànjié ma?	Christmas is an important holiday in my country. Do you celebrate Christmas?
STUDENT	Bú guò. Kěshì, Jīdūjiào jiàotáng huì yǒu qìngzhù huódòng.	No. But Christian churches have some celebrations in their churches.
MARK	Wǒ tīngshuōguo nǐmende "yuèbing." Nǐmen shénme shíhòu chī yuèbing?	I heard about your "mooncake." When do you eat it?
STUDENT	Wǒmen zài Zhōngqiūjié chī yuèbing.	We eat mooncakes on Mid-fall Festival.

Now see if you can match the holidays with the English words.

1. **Zhōngqiūjié**
2. **Duānwǔjié**
3. **Qīngmíngjié**
4. **Yuándàn**
5. **Láodòngjié**
6. **Guóqìngjié**
7. **Chūnjié**

a. Chinese New Year
b. Clear and Bright
c. Mid-fall Festival
d. National Day
e. New Year's Day
f. Dragon Boat Festival
g. Worker's Day

Túbùlǚxíng hé Pǎobù

Going on Hikes and Jogging

Mary Smith is in great shape. She jogs every morning. Sometimes she is joined by her husband and children, but they can barely keep up. This morning she is approached by a newspaper reporter who is writing an article on sports.

REPORTER	Zǎoshang hǎo. Wǒ shì jìzhě. Wǒ kéyǐ wèn nín jǐge wèntí ma?	Good morning. I am a reporter. May I ask you a few questions?
MARY	Qǐngwèn ba. Zhǐshì shuō màndiǎn. Wǒ shì ge Měiguórén. Hànyǔ dǒng de bùduō.	Please. Only speak slowly. I am an American and do not understand everything.
REPORTER	Nín jīngcháng pǎobù ma?	Do you jog often?
MARY	Wǒ měitiān zǎoshang pǎobù. Yǒushí wǒ zhàngfu hé háizi gēn wǒ yìqǐ pǎo.	I run every morning. Sometimes my husband and children run with me.
REPORTER	Zài Měiguó rénmen pǎobù dōu chuān xiē shénme?	What do people wear in America when they jog?
MARY	Wǒmen tōngcháng chuān yùndòngfú hé yùndòngxié.	Usually we wear a jogging suit and sneakers.

REPORTER	**Nǐmen hái xǐhuān shénme qítāde yùndòng?**	What other types of sports do you like?
MARY	**Wǒde yìjiārén díquè xǐhuān túbùlǚxíng.**	My family really likes to go on hikes.
REPORTER	**Nínde zhàngfu xǐhuān zài diànshì shàng kàn tǐyù jiému ma?**	Does your husband like to watch sports on television?
MARY	**Ò xǐhuān. Tā měige xīngqī liù kàn gǎnlǎnqiú huò lánqiú.**	Oh yes! He watches football or basketball every Saturday.
REPORTER	**Xièxie nínde shíjiān.**	Thank you for your time.

Qíchē yǔ Yóuyǒng
Bicycling and Swimming

qíchē
bicycle

yóuyǒng
swim

yóuyǒng yī
bathing suit

hùmùjìng
goggles

yǎngyǒng
backstroke

zìyóuyǒng
crawl

wāyǒng
breaststroke

xiūxi
rest

shàitàiyáng
sunbathe

Verbs with Zài

The word **zài** placed before a verb helps to express an action in progress.

Tā yóuyǒng.	→	He swims.
Tā zài yóuyǒng.	→	He is swimming.

The progressive action may be in the present, in the past, or in the future. It depends on the other words of time.

Wǒmen xiànzài zài tánhuà.	→	We are now talking.
Zuótiān tā qù yóuyǒng de shíhòu, wǒmen zài tánhuà.	→	When he went swimming yesterday, we were talking.

In the negative form, use **méi yǒu** before the verb in place of **zài**.

Tā méi yǒu yóuyǒng.	→	He is not swimming.
Wǒmen méi yǒu tánhuà.	→	We are not talking.

Before we go out to do some exercise, let's try to describe the following pictures, using the word **zài.**

1.

    _____

2.

    _____

3.

    _____

4.

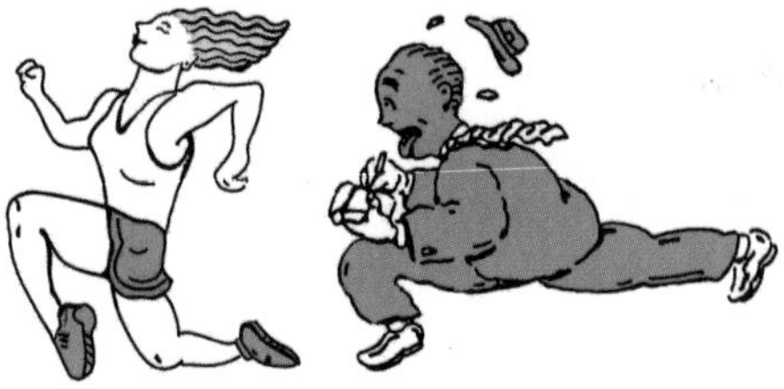

_____

5.

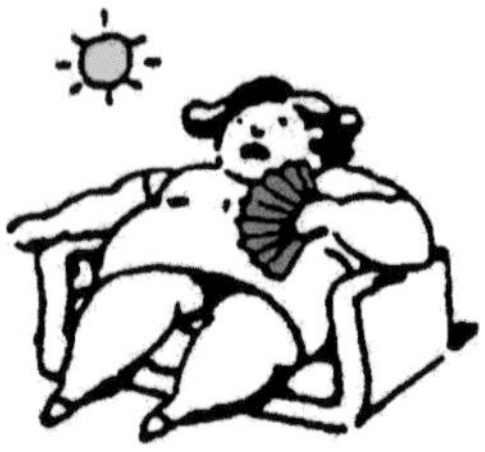

_____

14	**Zǎocan** Breakfast	**Wǔcān** Lunch	**Zhèngcān** Dinner

Chinese cuisine is no doubt one of the world's best. Be sure you don't miss any opportunities to taste authentic Chinese food while you are in China.

It's time to learn some expressions you might need when you eat out.

chī → eat
hē → drink
zǎocān → breakfast
wǔcān → lunch
wǎncān → supper
zhèngcān → dinner

Zǎocān
Breakfast

China has so many different cuisines, it's hard to tell what is a typical Chinese breakfast. But a breakfast of one or two **bāozi** (steamed bun with meat stuffing), some **huāshēngmǐ** (peanuts), a bowl of **zhōu** (rice gruel), and some **xiáncài** (pickles) would be authentic.

At most hotels in Beijing, Western-style breakfast is usually available. Mark and his family are now in their hotel dining room. Mary is helping her family to order.

MARY	**Nǐ zǎofàn xiǎng chī shénme?**	What do you want for breakfast?
MARK	**Wǒ xiǎng cháng diǎn bāozi. Nǐ ne?**	I want to try some baozi. And you?
MARY	**Wǒ yě chī yíge. Háizimen, nǐmen ne?**	I will take one, too. How about you, children?

PAUL	Wǒ xiǎng chī xiánròu hé jīdàn.	I prefer some bacon and eggs.
ANNE	Wǒ yě yíyàng. Jiā yí piàn kǎomiànbāo. Qǐng gěi wǒ yìbēi júzizhī, hǎoma?	I do, too. And a slice of toast. May I have a glass of orange juice, please?
PAUL	Wǒ xiǎng hē qiǎokèlì niúnǎi, hǎoma?	I want chocolate milk, please.
MARY	Hǎode. Nǐ yào kāfēi ma, Mǎkè?	OK. Do you want your coffee, Mark?
MARK	Yào.	Yes, I do.
WAITER	Nǐmen zhǔnbèi diǎn le ma?	Are you ready to order now?
MARY	Wǒmen zhǔnbèihǎo le.	Yes, we are.

Fill in the blanks according to the English given in parentheses.

1. Nǐ _____ xiǎng chī shénme? (What do you want for breakfast?)

2. Wǒ xiǎng _____ diǎn bāozi. (I want to try some baozi.)

3. Wǒ yě _____ yíge. (I will take one, too.)

4. Qǐng gěi wǒ _____, hǎoma? (May I have a glass of orange juice, pl)

5. Wǒ xiǎng hē qiǎokèlì niúnǎi, _____? (I want chocolate milk, please.)

6. Nǐ _____ kāfēi ma? (Do you want your coffee?)

7. Nǐmen _____ diǎn le ma? (Are you ready to order now?)

Cānzhuō
The Table

jiǔbēi
wine glass

bōlíbēi
glass

chábēi
cup

yán hé hújiāo
salt and pepper

táng
sugar

cānjīn
napkin

kuàizi
chopsticks

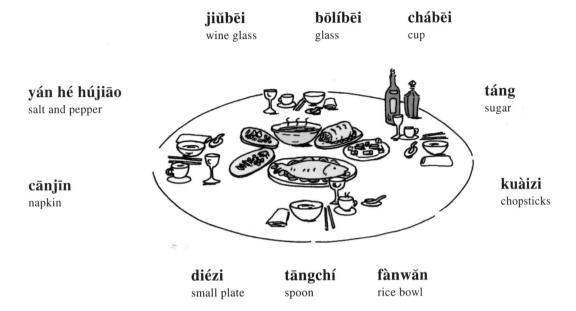

diézi
small plate

tāngchí
spoon

fànwǎn
rice bowl

Wǔcān
Lunch

The main meal of the day for Chinese can be **wǔcān** (lunch) or **zhèngcān** (dinner). It depends. Nowadays, most people who work during the day do not have much time for a big meal at lunch. Usually they would have a quick lunch and enjoy a big meal in the evening.

A typical light lunch for Chinese would be a bowl of noodles (there are many varieties) with some meat and vegetables. Some people may have a bowl or two of fried rice similar to the kind served in Chinese restaurants in the United States.

Following are a few items you can order for a light lunch.

Wǒ xiǎng yào yìwǎn . . .		I'd like to have a bowl of . . .
niúròu	**miàn**	noodles with beef
jīròu	**miàn**	noodles with chicken
xiā	**miàn**	noodles with shrimp
xiāngcháng	**miàn**	noodles with sausages
qīngtāng	**miàn**	noodles only
Qǐng gěi wǒ yìbēi . . .		Please give me a glass (cup) of . . .
píjiǔ		beer
kělè		coke
shuǐ		water
chá		tea
kāfēi		coffee

Zhèngcān

Dinner

A dinner normally consists of four or five dishes and a bowl of soup. The dishes can be anything from meat, poultry, freshwater fish, shrimp, and fresh vegetables.

Look at the picture below and see if you can find the following items.

kāiwèipin
appetizers

tāng
soup

jiǔ
wine

shūcài
vegetables

yú
fish

liángcài
side dishes/cold dishes

shuǐguǒ
fruits

ròu
meat

Let's see if we can remember some of the important words from our dining experiences.

1. What are the three meals of the day?

_____ ,

_____ ,

_____ .

2. Think of something you would like for a light lunch and write it down:

(for food) _____

(for drink) _____

3. Without looking at the pictures, match up the two columns.

1. **jiǔbēi**	a. chopsticks
2. **bōlíbēi**	b. cup
3. **chábēi**	c. glass
4. **yán hé hújiāo**	d. napkin
5. **táng**	e. rice bowl
6. **cānjīn**	f. salt and pepper
7. **kuàizi**	g. small plate
8. **diézi**	h. spoon
9. **tāngchí**	i. sugar
10. **fànwǎn**	j. wine glass

93

As the capital of the nation, Beijing serves as a center for almost everything, even food. The four best-known Chinese cuisines and many others are represented in Beijing's restaurants. You should eat at a local restaurant, both for atmosphere and the great authenticity in their preparations, and for their wide array of offerings.

China is one of the few countries where you don't have to tip when you eat out.

Qǐng ná Càidān
The Menu, Please

At a restaurant, remember the following expressions:

cháng → taste; try the flavor of . . .

diǎncài → order (from the menu)

shàngcài → bring (the food)

Qǐng bǎ . . . gěi wǒ → Please bring me . . .

Wǒ yào . . . → I'll take . . .

kāiwèipǐn	appetizers	**liángcài**	side dishes
lěngdié	cold dishes	**dìèr dào cài**	second (course)
rècài	hot dishes	**yú**	fish
dìyī dào cài	first (course)	**ròu**	meat
tāng	soup	**jī**	chicken
		shūcài	vegetables
		shuǐguǒ	fruits
		dìsān dào cài	third (course)
		tiándiǎn	dessert (sweets)
		yǐnliào	beverages

Mary and Mark have decided to have dinner in a fine local restaurant. After they have been seated and have looked at the menu, a waiter comes to the table.

WAITER	**Wǎnshang hǎo. Nǐmen xiǎng chī shénme?**	Good evening. What would you like from the menu?
MARK	**Jīntiānde tècài shì shénme?**	What's today's special?
WAITER	**Rúguǒ nǐmen xǐhuān chī yú, wǒmen yǒu qīngzhēng jìyú, tángcù lǐyú, hé jiācháng huángyú.**	If you like fish, we have steamed crucian carp, sweet-and-sour carp, and home-style yellow croaker.
MARY	**Wǒmen yào tángcù lǐyú. Qítāde ròushí ne?**	We'll take the sweet-and-sour carp. What about other meat?
WAITER	**Wǒmen yǒu hóngshāo niúròu, xiāngwèi ròudīng, hé kòuròu.**	We have beef braised in brown sauce, spiced diced pork, and stewed-fried steamed pork.
MARK	**Wǒmen yào hóngshāo niúròu.**	We'll take the beef braised in brown sauce.
WAITER	**Nǐmen xiǎng chī shénme shūcài?**	What vegetables would you like?
MARY	**Wǒmen xiǎng cháng diǎnr dàbáicài.**	I want to try some Chinese cabbage.
WAITER	**Hǎode. Nǐmen xiǎng yào tiántāng ma?**	OK. Would you like some sweet soup?
MARK	**Duì. Nǐmen yǒu dòufu ma?**	Yes. Do you have tofu?
WAITER	**Yǒu. Nǐmen xiǎng yào yìpán ma?**	Yes. Would you like to order one?

MARY	Yào yìpán.	Yes. We'll take one.
WAITER	**Nǐmen xiǎng hē diǎnr shénme?** Xiǎng bù xiǎng cháng diǎn Zhōngguóde jiǔ? **Máotáijiǔ shì zuì hǎode.**	What would you like to drink? Would you like to try some Chinese wine/liquor? Maotai is the best.

MARK	**Wǒmen tīngshuō le.** Wǒmen zhǐshì cháng yìdiǎn. **Qǐng gěi wǒ yì bēi kělè jiā bīngkuàir.**	We heard of it. We'll just try a little of it. Would you please bring me a coke with ice?
WAITER	**Hǎode.**	Sure.
MARY	Wǒ yào **níngméngchá.**	I want tea with lemon, please.
WAITER	**Hǎode. Tiándiǎn, wǒmen yǒu shuǐguǒ hé qiǎokèlì dàngāo.**	OK. For dessert, we have fruit and some chocolate cake.
MARY	Wǒmen yào qiǎokèlì dàngāo.	We'll take chocolate cake.
WAITER	**Nǐmen yào kāfēi háishì yào chá?**	Do you want coffee or tea with it?
MARK	Yào kāfēi.	Coffee, please.
WAITER	Xièxie. Wǒ xiān gěi nǐmen shàng kāiwèipǐn.	Thank you. I'll bring your appetizer first.

Cèsuǒ Zài Nǎr?

Where Is the Restroom?

After their meal, Mark and Mary both want to freshen up.

nǚ cèsuǒ
ladies

nán cèsuǒ
men

Read back over the dialogue between the waiter and Mary and Mark. Let's see what they ordered for their dinner. Write down the items they ordered in the spaces provided.

Fish   _____

Meat   _____

Vegetables   _____

                _____

Soup   _____

Drinks   _____

                _____

                _____

                _____

Dessert   _____

It's finally time for Mary and Mark to pay for their meal.

MARK	**Qǐng bǎ zhàngdān gěi wǒmen.**	Please bring us the check.
WAITER	**Zài zhèr.**	Here it is.
MARK	**Měiyíyàng cài dōu hěn hǎo chī.**	Everything was delicious.
	Qǐng nǐ bāng wǒmen fù yíxià	Would you help us pay the check?
	zhàngdān, hǎoma? Zhè shì qián.	Here is the money.
WAITER	**Hǎode.**	Sure.

(Waiter comes back with some change.)

MARY	**Xièxie. Zhèdiǎn qián nǐ liúzhe.**	Thank you. Keep the change.
WAITER	**Búyòngle. Wǒmen bù shōu xiǎofèi. Zài Zhōngguó nǐ búyòng fù xiǎofèi.**	No, thanks. We don't take tips. In China, you don't have to tip.
MARY	**Wèishénme? Wǒmen chīde hǎo, yě gǎnxiè nǐde fúwù. Wǒmen xiǎng yào nǐ shōuxià.**	Why? We enjoyed our dinner and appreciate your service. We'd love for you to have it.
WAITER	**Nǐmen tài kègile. Wǒ Xièxie nǐmen.**	That's very kind of you. I thank you.

Although in most restaurants tips are not expected, they are appreciated.

Qǐng Suíbiàn Chī!

Help Yourself!

Read the preceding dialogue again. Try to pick out something you might like for dinner.

Fish	_____	_____
Meat	_____	_____
Vegetables	_____	_____
Soup	_____	_____
Dessert	_____	_____
Drinks	_____	_____

HOW ARE WE DOING?

Wǒmen Xuéde Zěnyàng?

We're already halfway through the book. Now let's take a break and do some exercises to see how well we are doing. We have covered a lot of ground. This section gives you a chance to reinforce what you have learned through the first 15 chapters.

Now let's begin!

Can you read the following Chinese signs? Look at them carefully and then write the meaning for each sign in the space next to it.

1. 　　　　　　　　　　_____

2. 　　　　　　　　　　_____

3. 　　　　　　　　　　_____

4. 　　　　　　　　　　_____

5. 　　　　　　　　　　_____

Sometimes we want to sound more diplomatic. The expressions in column B are more polite than the ones in column A. Try to match them.

<u>A</u>	<u>B</u>
1. **Nǐ zǎo.** (Good morning.)	a. **Búyào xīyān ba!**
2. **Jìnlai.** (Come in.)	b. **Nín zǎo.**
3. **Qǐng zuòxià.** (Please sit down.)	c. **Qǐng jìnlai.**
4. **Búyào xīyān!** (Don't smoke!)	d. **Qǐng nín zuòxià.**
5. **Jǐ diǎn le?** (What time is it?)	e. **Qǐngwèn jǐ diǎn le?**

Let's see how well you remember your numbers in Chinese. Do the following simple mathematical equations and fill in the blanks with the written forms of the numerals.

1. 2 _____ + (jiā) 5 _____ = **děngyú** _____

2. 5 _____ + (jiā) 3 _____ = **děngyú** _____

3. 6 _____ – (jiǎn) 4 _____ = **děngyú** _____

4. 8 _____ – (jiǎn) 7 _____ = **děngyú** _____

5. 4 _____ + (jiā) 6 _____ = **děngyú** _____

Now look at the clocks and tell the time. Write down your answers in the spaces provided.

1.

_____

2.

_____

3.

_____

4.

_____

5.

_____

6.

_____

100

Do you recognize the flags? Write the Chinese name of the country.

1.

         _____ .

2.

         _____ .

3.

         _____ .

4.

         _____ .

5.

         _____ .

6.

         _____ .

7.

         _____ .

8.

         _____ .

9.

         _____ .

10.

         _____ .

What's the weather like according to the pictures? Write down your answers.

1.

         _____

2.

         _____

3. 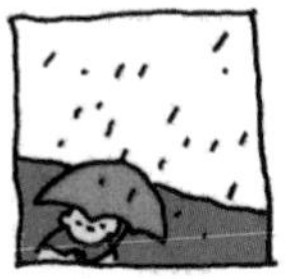 ____________________

4. 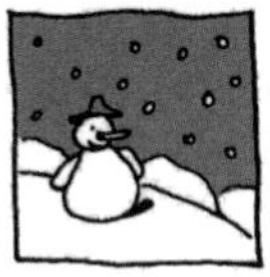 ____________________

Do you recognize what our friends are doing for recreation? Try to describe the following pictures, using the word **zài** in each sentence.

1. ______________________________ 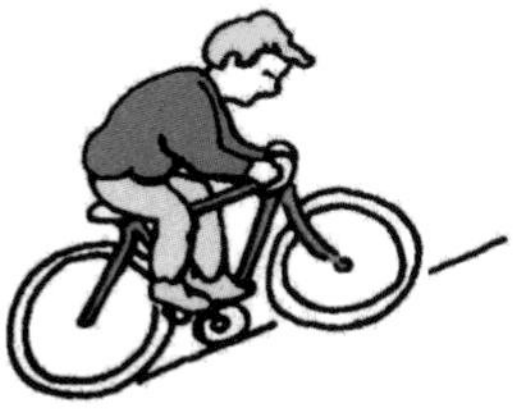

2. ______________________________ 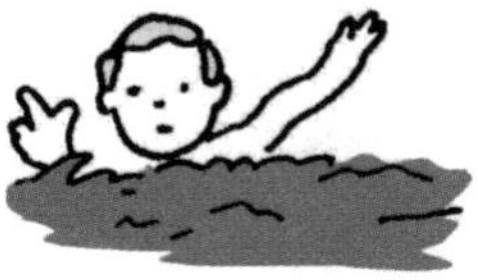

3. ______________________________ 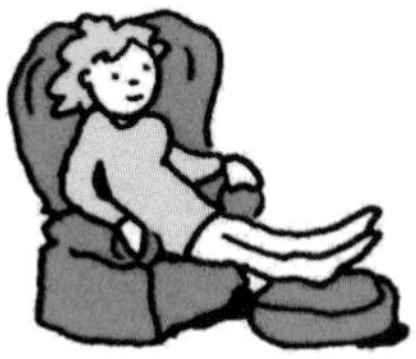

4. ______________________________ 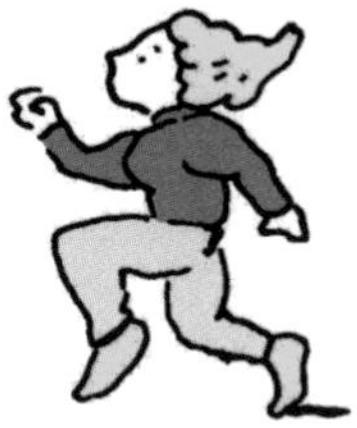

5. ______________________________ 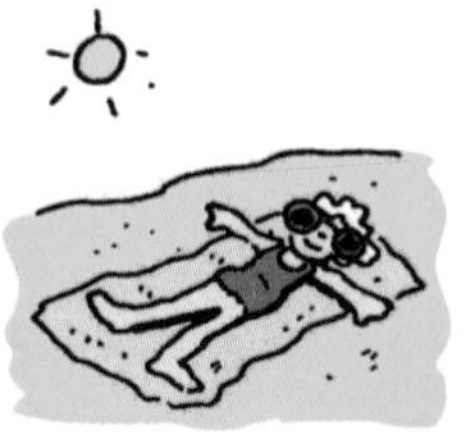

ANSWERS

Weather **3.** Zài xiàyǔ. **4.** Zài xiàxuě.

Exercise **1.** Mǎkè zài qíchē. **2.** Bǎoluó zài yóuyǒng. **3.** Tā zài xiūxi. **4.** Mǎlì zài pǎobù. **5.** Ānní zài shàitàiyáng.

Look at the picture of the table and try to find as many words in the puzzle as you can.

Cānzhuō
The Table

jiǔbēi
wine glass

bōlíbēi
glass

chábēi
cup

yán hé hújiāo
salt and pepper

táng
sugar

cānjīn
napkin

kuàizi
chopsticks

diézi
small plate

tāngchí
spoon

fànwǎn
rice bowl

F	P	W	G	F	N	A	Y	O	J	M	Y
U	I	N	P	O	C	A	I	E	G	L	M
Q	A	Z	L	S	J	H	J	Y	Y	B	A
T	F	T	I	P	O	I	A	U	Z	F	G
E	X	N	A	A	B	U	U	B	F	C	N
P	H	E	A	N	U	O	H	B	E	F	I
D	D	U	F	W	G	K	L	Z	E	I	M
T	J	I	J	C	N	C	C	I	N	I	O
Q	O	F	E	I	H	A	H	A	B	A	G
L	T	I	Q	Z	A	J	F	I	N	E	C
A	S	E	S	C	I	O	H	J	S	J	I
T	U	T	F	O	N	F	C	I	D	O	I

AT THE STORE
Zài Shāngdiàn

16	**Fúzhuāng, Chǐmǎ, Yánsè**
	Clothing Sizes Colors

Tā zài chuān yīfu.
He is getting dressed.

Tā zài chuān chènyī.
He is putting on his shirt.

Tā zài tuō yīfu.
She is undressing.

Tā zài tuō chènqún.
She is taking off her slip.

Nǐ Suǒ Xūyào Zhīdao De
What You Need to Know

In most shops in China you will first want to examine the articles with the help of the salesperson behind the counter. You may want to ask them to show you an item—**Qǐng bǎ . . . gěi wǒ kàn kan.** (Show me . . ., please). You may want to try something on—**Wǒ kéyǐ shìchuān yíxià ma?** (May I try it on?). Then you will need to find out the price—**Zhè jiàn duōshǎo qián?** (How much does it cost?). When you have finally decided on your purchase, the salesperson will write you up and you must go to the cashier and pay there. The cashier will give you a receipt **(shōujù)** that you bring back to the original counter where your purchase will be waiting for you. If you smile and show courtesy and good humor, you are likely to be helped through the process.

Nánshì Fúzhuāng
Men's Clothing

wàzi
socks

xuēzi
boots

pídài
belt

dàyī
overcoat

lǐngdài
necktie

chènyī
shirt

nèikù
underpants

shǒupà
handkerchief

máoyī
sweater

biànkù
slacks

wàitào
sport coat

hànshān
T shirt

yǔsǎn
umbrella

tàozhuāng
suit

màozi
hat

shǒutào
gloves

Words that mean "wear, put on, and take off"

In Chinese we use different words for wearing or putting on different things. The same is true for the expressions for taking off. Learn the following list of words.

chuān   wear, put on (clothes such as jacket, pants, shirt, etc.)
tuō   take off (clothes such as jacket, pants, shirt, etc.)
dài   wear, put on (hat, cap, watch, ring, earring, glasses, contact lens, etc.)
zhāi   take off (hat, cap, watch, ring, earring, glasses, contact lens, etc.)

Sometimes **shàng** is used after **chuān** and **dài** to show the completion of the action; in the same way, **xià** is used after **tuō** and **zhāi**.

Tā chuānshàng yīfu.	He put on the clothes.
Tā tuōxià chènyī.	He took off the shirt.
Wǒ dàishàng màozi.	I put on my hat.
Wǒ zhāixià màozi.	I took off my hat.

Mark is invited to go to a party. He needs some clothes for the party. Let's see how he does at the department store.

CLERK	**Nín xūyào mǎi shénme?**	How may I help you, sir?
MARK	**Wǒ xūyào yítào xīn xīzhuāng, yíjiàn chènyī, yìtiáo lǐngdài hé jǐshuāng wàzi.**	I need a new suit, a shirt, a tie, and some socks.
CLERK	**Hǎode. Nín chuān jǐhào de xīzhuāng?**	Fine. What size suit do you wear?
MARK	**Sìshi èr.**	42.
CLERK	**Nín xǐhuān shénme yánsè de?**	What color do you like, sir?
MARK	**Shēn lánsè de.**	Navy blue.

CLERK	Hǎode. **Nín juéde zhè yítào zěnmeyàng?**	OK. How about this one?
MARK	**Wǒ kéyǐ shìchuān yíxià ma?**	May I try it on?
CLERK	Dāngrán kéyǐ. Shìyījiān zài nèibiān.	Certainly. The fitting room is over there.

(In front of the mirror)

CLERK	Qiáo, nín chuān zhètào duō héshēn.	Look how well it fits!
MARK	**Wǒ yě shì zhème xiǎng de.**	I think so too.
CLERK	**Wǒ dài nín qù kàn chènyī hé lǐngdài. Qǐng zhè biān zǒu.** Nín xǐhuān zhè yíjiàn chènyī hé zhè yìtiáo lǐngdài ma?	Let me show you some shirts and ties. This way, please. Do you like this shirt and this tie?
MARK	Hái xíng ba. **Zǒnggòng duōshǎo qián?**	I think I do. How much are all these?
CLERK	Wǒ mǎshàng wèi nín suàn chūlai. Zǒnggòng shì yì qiān yuán.	I'll figure it out for you in a minute. The total is one thousand *yuan*.
MARK	Hǎode. **Wǒ dōu yào.**	OK. I'll take all of them.
CLERK	**Qǐng nín bǎ zhàngdān ná dào shōukuǎnchù, zài nàbiān fùkuǎn.** Nín fù wán kuǎn, wǒ jiù wèi nín bāohǎo le.	If you will take this bill to the cashier and pay there, I'll wrap them up for you when you are ready.
MARK	Xièxie.	Thank you.

Xiézi
Shoes

Zhè xié tài zhǎi le.
They are too narrow.

Zhè xié jiā jiǎo.

They pinch me.

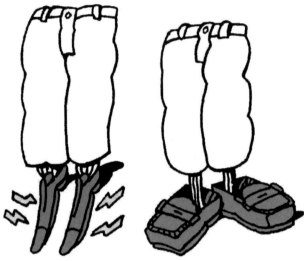

Zhè xié tài dà le.
They are too large.

Zhè xié wǒ chuān tài kuān.
They're too wide for me.

píxuē
boots

gāogēnxié
high-heeled shoes

qiúxié
sneakers

Nǔshì Fúzhuāng
Women's Clothing

Jībén Yánsè
Basic Colors

huáng xiōngzhào
yellow bra

hēi shǒutíbāo
black handbag

dànlánsè lǐfú
light blue dress

shēn lánsè wéijīn
dark blue scarf

huáng nèikù
yellow panties

bái chènqún
white slip

lǜ chènyī
green blouse

hóng qúnzi
red skirt

You and a friend are going to a party and want some clothes that really stand out. Write out your order beforehand and then tell the shopkeeper exactly what you need.

Wǒ yào mǎi xià liè yīwù:

1. a yellow blouse _____

2. a green tie _____

3. a light blue jacket _____

4. dark blue pants _____

5. red boots _____

6. a black skirt _____

ANSWERS

Clothes   1. yíjiàn huáng chènyī   2. yìtiáo lǜ lǐngdài   3. yíjiàn dànlánsè shàngzhuāng   4. shēn lánsè kùzi   5. hóng píxuē   6. yìtiáo hēi qúnzi

Shopping for food can be another pleasurable experience during your stay in China. Here are some helpful words. Chinese use **diàn** after the food words to mean a store or shop for that kind of food. For instance, **ròu** means "meat," **ròu diàn** means "butcher's shop."

niúnǎi	**ròu**	**shūcài**	**shuǐguǒ**	**miànbāo**
milk	meat	vegetables	fruits	bread

yú	**tángguǒ**	**gāodiǎn**	**bīngqílín**	**jiǔ**
fish	candy	pastry	ice cream	wine

Tài Duō Wèntí
Too Many Questions

Mark and Mary approach a **jǐngchá** (policeman).

MARK	**Wǒmen kéyǐ wènwen nǐ ma?**	May we ask you something?
POLICEMAN	**Kéyǐ.**	I'm listening.
MARK	**Wǒmen zài shénme dìfāng mǎi miànbāo?**	Where can we buy bread?
POLICEMAN	**Zhè tiáojiē shàng yǒu yìjiā miànbāodiàn.**	There is a bakery on this street.

110

MARY	Wŏmen zài năr néng măidào **xiāngbīnjiŭ** ne?	Where can we buy champagne?
POLICEMAN	Zài jiŭdiàn.	In a liquor store.
MARK	Shūcài hé shuǐguǒ zài năr ne?	Where are the vegetables and fruits?
POLICEMAN	Zài càichăng.	At the food market.
MARY	Wŏmen zài năr néng măidào **niúròu hé zhūròu** ne?	Where can we find beef and pork?
POLICEMAN	Zài ròudiàn li.	At the butcher's.
MARK	Wŏ xǐhuān chī dàngāo. Zài nar . . .?	I love cake. Where is . . . ?
POLICEMAN	Zài gāodiăndiàn li.	In the pastry shop.
MARY	Kāfēi, chá, qìshuǐ háiyǒu jiŭ zài năr mai?	And where is the coffee, and the tea, and the soda, and the wine?
POLICEMAN	**Wèntí tài duō le.** Wŏ xiăng **nǐmen xūyào qù liăng gè dìfāng:** **fùshídiàn hé càichăng.**	Too many questions. I think you need to go to two places: the grocery and the food market.
MARK	Kěshì, zài năr . . .?	But, where...?
POLICEMAN	**Wŏ kàn wŏ zuì hăo dài nǐmen qù.**	I think I'd better take you there.
MARY	Nín zhēn shì tài hăo le.	That's very kind of you.

Please help Mark and Mary to go to the right place for their needs. Write down your answers in the spaces provided.

Tāmen yīnggāi qù (They should go to)

1. _____ **mǎi** (to buy) **miànbāo**

2. _____ **mǎi** (to buy) **xiāngbīnjiǔ**

3. _____ **mǎi** (to buy) **shūcài hé shuǐguǒ**

4. _____ **mǎi** (to buy) **niúròu hé zhūròu**

5. _____ **mǎi** (to buy) **dàngāo**

6. _____ **mǎi** (to buy) **kāfēi, chá, hé qìshuǐ**

Zhè Yǒu Duō Zhòng?

How Much Does It Weigh?

Although the metric system is widely used for measurements in China and in other countries and has become increasingly more familiar to Americans, it is still useful to learn the following when you travel abroad.

100 kè	100 grams = 3.5 ounces
200 kè	200 grams = 7 ounces (almost 1/2 pound)
500 kè	500 grams, half a kilo = 17.5 ounces (one pound + 1.5 ounces)
1000 kè	1000 grams, one kilogram = 2.205 pounds
1 shēng	1 liter = 1.06 quarts

ANSWERS

1. miànbāodiàn 2. jiǔdiàn 3. càichǎng 4. ròudiàn 5. gāodiǎndiàn 6. fùshídiàn

Zhè Yào Duōshǎo Qián?

How Much Does It Cost?

Read aloud the names of the different food amounts and containers.

yíkuài féizào
a bar of soap

yìpíng kāfēi
a jar of coffee

shí gè jīdàn
ten eggs

yìshēng niúnǎi
a liter of milk

yídài miànfěn
a bag of flour

yíkuài nǎilào
a piece of cheese

yìhé tángguǒ
a box of candy

yì juǎn shǒuzhǐ
a roll of toilet paper

yì tiáo miànbāo
a loaf of bread

yídài táng
a bag of sugar

yìpíng pútáojiǔ
a bottle of wine

yì gōngjīn tǔdòu
a kilogram of potatoes

Let's see if you can ask the clerk for the following items and ask how much each of them costs. **Zhè yào duōshǎo qián?** (How much does it cost?)

Qǐng gěi wǒ (Please give me . . .)

1. _____ (a bottle of wine).

2. _____ (a bar of soap).

3. _____ (a bag of sugar).

4. _____ (a kilogram of beef).

5. _____ (a package of tea).

Shìchǎng

The Market

One place you should not overlook in your shopping is the **shìchǎng.** These marketplaces are almost always better stocked than the stores, and they offer a feast of sights and smells. The local farmers are eager to sell their wares and will enter into lively conversations as they let you sample their goods. Be sure to bring a plastic or net bag to carry home your purchases. Chinese use a basket to do their grocery shopping.

Wǒ Gāi Wǎng Nǎr Zǒu?

Where Must I Go?

Look at the map below. Mark is at the ice-cream shop. Let's show him the way to get the items in this order: (1) bread, (2) apple, (3) fish.

These expressions will help.

Yìzhí zǒu.	Go straight ahead.
Yòu guǎi.	Turn right.
Zuǒ guǎi.	Turn left.
Guò yì tiáojiē.	Go across one street.
liǎng	two streets
Xiàng dōng zǒu.	Go east.
nán	south
xī	west
běi	north

1. From the ice cream shop to the bakery

   _____. _____.

2. Then from the bakery to the fruit stand.

   _____. _____.

3. From the fruit stand to the fishmarket.

   _____. _____.

   _____. _____.

An American drugstore is different from a Chinese drugstore (**yàodiàn**), which is actually a pharmacy. It carries mainly traditional Chinese medicine and some nonprescription medicine. Your prescription is often filled at the pharmacy of the hospital where you see your doctor. Take a supply of your prescription medicines with you to China as they may not be available there.

The **yàodiàn** also carries some personal care products. You can find Western cosmetics, toiletries, and medicines in drugstores in the arcades of most major hotels.

Let's take a look at some of the names for frequently needed items.

yáshuā
toothbrush

yágāo
toothpaste

zhǐjīn
tissues

kǒuhóng
lipstick

fàshuā
hairbrush

jìngzi
mirror

shūzi
comb

fàjiāo
hairspray

jiémáoyóu
mascara

zhǐjiayóu qùchújì
nail polish remover

Wèishēngjiānyòngpǐn Bù
The Toiletries Section

MARY	**Wǒ xūyào mǎi miànshuāng.**	I need some face cream.
ANNE	**Mā, nǐ zuótiān cái mǎi de huàzhuāngpǐn.**	You bought some makeup yesterday, Mom.
MARY	**Wǒ zhīdao. Kěshì wǒ bù xǐhuān nàxiē.**	I know, but I did not like it.
	Wǒ yě xūyào mǎi yìxiē qítāde dōngxī.	I need to pick up some other things, too.
CLERK	**Nín xūyào mǎi diǎn shénme?**	May I help you?
MARY	**Wǒ xūyào mǎi miànshuāng hé yānzhi.**	Yes. I need some face cream and rouge.
CLERK	**Hǎode. Wǒmen yǒu hěnduō pǐnzhǒng, nín kéyǐ tiāoxuǎn.**	All right. We have a lot of items that you can choose.
MARY	**Nà hǎo. Wǒ hái xūyào mǎi yícìxìng wèishēngdài hé shuǎngshēnfěn.**	Oh, good. I also need to buy some disposable diapers and talcum.
CLERK	**Méi wèntí. Wǒmen zhèr yě mài.**	No problem. We carry them here too.
MARY	**Xiāngshuǐ ne?**	How about perfume?

CLERK	**Wǒmen jì yǒu guóchǎnde**	We have both home-made
	yě yǒu jìnkǒude.	and imported brands.
MARY	**Nà tàihǎo le.**	That's good.

Yìdiǎn Yǔfǎ
Some Grammar

Elliptical questions with **ne.**

Elliptical questions may be formed by adding the modal particle **ne** to a noun or a pronoun. The meaning of this kind of question is determined by the context. Read again the dialogue at the breakfast table when the Smiths are trying to decide what to order.

MARK	**Wǒ xiǎng cháng diǎn bāozi.**	I want to try some baozi.
	Nǐ ne?	And you?
MARY	**Wǒ yě chī yígè.**	I will take one, too.
	Háizimen, nǐmen ne?	How about you, children?

When Mark said **"Nǐ ne?"** he meant: **"Nǐ xiǎng cháng diǎn bāozi ma?"**
When Mary said **"Háizimen, nǐmen ne?"** she was saying: **"Nǐmen yě chī bāozi ma?"**

Bìbèipǐn
Necessary Items

Write the names of these important items in the spaces provided.

chúchòujì
deodorant

_____

diàndòng tìxūdāo
electric shaver

_____

tìxūdāopiàn
razor blades

_____

tìxūdāo
razor

_____

118

Mark Smith and Li Feng, a Chinese friend, are at a drugstore.

MARK	**Wǒde diàndòng tìxūdāo huài le.**	My electric shaver doesn't work.
LI FENG	**Nà jiù mǎi yìbǎ tìxūdāo hé yìxiē tìxūdāopiàn.**	Buy a razor and some blades, then.
MARK	**Nà hěn máfan.** Yòu shì tìxūgāo yòu shì xiāngshuǐ.	That's too much work. Shaving cream, aftershave.
LI FENG	**Duì. Kěshì shénme dìfāng dōu néng yòng.**	Yes. But it works everywhere.
MARK	**Nǐ shuōde duì.** Yěxǔ wǒ zhēnde gāi mǎi yìbǎ. Wǒ yě xūyào mǎi jǐkuài féizào hé xǐfàjīng.	You're right. Maybe I really should buy one. I also need to get some soap and shampoo.
LI FENG	**Nǐ hái xūyào mǎi kēlóngxiāngshuǐ ma?**	Do you need to buy cologne?
MARK	**Bùxūyào. Wǒ hái yǒu yìxiē.**	I still have some.

Zài Yàodiàn
At the Pharmacy

If you are sick and need some over-the-counter medicine, the following expressions will help. Just put in a name of the illness or the symptom in the blank.

To ask for items you need, you can simply say:

Wǒ xūyào yìdiǎn zhì _____ **de yào.**   **Wǒ yào mǎi** _____.

I need some medicine for _____ .   I want to buy _____.

gǎnmào
a cold

biànbì
constipation

késou
a cough

fùxiè
diarrhea

fāshāo
a fever

tóutòng
a headache

ěxīn
nausea

liúgǎn
the flu

yátòng
a toothache

wèitòng
an upset stomach

zhǐxiěsāi
tampons

kàngsuānjì
an antacid

jiǔjīng
alcohol

kàngjūnjì
an antiseptic

āsīpīlín
aspirin

bēngdài
bandages

miánqiú
cotton

yǎnyàoshuǐ
eyedrops

diǎndīng
iodine

tǐwēnjì
a thermometer

Let's make sure you can describe your symptoms and get what you need. First match the Chinese names for some symptoms with the English equivalents.

1. gǎnmào		a. a cold
2. biànbì		b. a fever
3. késou		c. a headache
4. fùxiè		d. a toothache
5. fāshāo		e. constipation
6. tóutòng		f. a cough
7. ěxīn		g. diarrhea
8. liúgǎn		h. nausea
9. yátòng		i. the flu
10. wèitòng		j. an upset stomach

Here is your shopping list. Can you translate the items into Chinese for the cashier?

1. an antacid   _____

2. alcohol   _____

3. an antiseptic   _____

4. bandages   _____

5. a thermometer   _____

6. shampoo   _____

7. deodorant   _____

8. face cream   _____

9. toothpaste   _____

10. rouge   _____

ANSWERS

Matching 1. a 2. e 3. f 4. g 5. b 6. c 7. h 8. i 9. d 10. j

Shopping list 1. kàngsuānjì 2. jiǔjīng 3. kàngjūnjì 4. bēngdài 5. tǐwēnjì 6. xǐfàjīng 7. chúchòujì 8. miànshuāng 9. yágāo 10. yānzhī

xǐ
to wash

chōngxǐ
to rinse

hōnggān
to dry

tàng
to iron

You may be able to have your shirts, blouses, and underwear washed at the hotel for a modest price. There will also probably be an ironing board and iron on your floor. Simply ask the maid. Or you may want to try out the laundromat and dry cleaner's.

xǐyīdiàn
laundromat

xǐyifěn
detergent

yùndǒu
iron

tàngyībǎn
ironing board

xǐyījī
washing machine

hōnggānjī
dryer

Bīnguǎn De Xǐyī hé Gānxǐ Fúwù
Hotel Laundry and Dry Cleaning Service

You will probably want to use the laundry services of the hotel where you stay. These expressions may be useful.

Nǐmen yǒu xǐyī fúwù ma?	Do you have a laundry service?
Wǒ yǒu xiē yīfu yào xǐ.	I have some clothes to be washed.
Qǐng dìng shàng zhèkē kòuzi.	Please sew on the button.
Nǐ néng bǔbu zhèzhī xiùzi ma?	Can you mend this sleeve?
Nǐ néng tàng yí tàng zhè jiàn chènyī ma?	Can you iron this shirt?
Wǒ bù xiǎng jiāng wǒde chènyī.	I don't want any starch in my shirt.
Nǐ néng bǎ wǒde xīzhuāng sòngqu gānxǐ ma?	Could you have my suit dry cleaned?
Nǐ néng chúdiào zhège wūdiǎn ma?	Can you remove this stain?

Now fill in the blanks using the words and expressions found above.

1. **Qǐng** _____ **zhèke** _____ .
              sew on   button.

2. **Nǐ néng** _____ **zhèzhī** _____ **ma?**
                 mend   sleeve

3. **Nǐ néng** _____ **zhè jiàn** _____ **ma?**
                 iron   shirt

4. **Nǐ néng bǎ wǒde** _____ **sòngqu** _____ **ma?**
                         suit   dry cleaned

5. **Nǐ néng** _____ **zhèdiǎn** _____ **ma?**
               remove   stain

Bàoyuàn
Complaints

Măkè **zŏngshì** bă yīfu sòngdào
bīnguăn xǐyīfáng qù. Tāmen
tōngcháng fúwù de fēichánghăo.
Zhèyícì chū le wèntí.
Tā náhuí de nèiyī
shì biérén de.
Măkè xiàng fúwùyuán bàoyuàn.
Tā **cóngbù** chuān nǚshì
nèiyī.
Tāde liăngzhī wàzi bújiàn le, yìzhī
hóngsè de, lìngyìzhī shì lùsè de.
Tāde chènyī shàng
shàngle tàiduō de jiāng.
Gāng cóng gānxǐdiàn
náhuíde xīzhuāng
shàng háiyŏu **wūdiăn.**
Măkè hěn shēngqì.
Nín juéde ne?
Tā yŏu zhíde bàoyuànde
shì ma?

Mark always sends his clothes
to the hotel laundry service.
They usually do an excellent job.
This time there are problems.
The underwear he received
belong to another person.
Mark complains to the maid.
He never wears women's
underwear.
His two socks are missing,
one red, the other green.

His shirts have too much
starch.
There was still a stain on the
suit he just received from the
cleaner's.

Mark is very angry.
What do you think?
Does he have something
to complain about?

Here are some useful phrases if you have a complaint.

Wǒ yào xiàng jīnglǐ fǎnyìngqíngkuàng.
I'm going to complain to the manager.

Yìkē kòuzi diào le.
A button is missing.

Yīfu méiyǒu dié.
The clothes are not folded.

Wǒde chènyī xǐ huài le.
My blouse is ruined.

Yíjiàn nèiyī bújiàn le.
An undershirt is missing.

Qúnzi yě méiyǒu tàng.
The skirt is not ironed.

Can you fill in the blanks corresponding to the pictures?

1. **Xīzhuāng shàng yǒu** _____.

2. **Wǒ cóngbù chuān** _____.

3. **Yìkē** _____ **diào le.**

4. _____ **méiyǒu tàng.**

5. **Tāde liǎngzhī wàzi bújiàn le,** _____.

125

Měiróngdiàn
Beauty Salon

tóufa
hair

cháng
long

duǎn
short

qiǎnhēisè
brunette

jīnsè
blond

xǐfà
shampoo

fàshuā
brush

tóufashìyàng
hairdo

lǐfà
haircut

dìngxíng
set

shūtóu
to comb

xiūzhǐjia
manicure

miànmó
facial massage

fàjiāo
hairspray

fàjuǎn
rollers

hōngfàzhào
hair dryer

jiǎndāo
scissors

Mary and Anne decide to go to a beauty shop.

HAIRDRESSER	**Nǐmen yào zěnyàng lǐfà?**	What can I do for you?
ANNE	**Wǒ xiǎng xǐfà, jiǎn yìdiǎn ránhòu dìngxíng.**	I'd like a shampoo, a cut, and then set.
HAIRDRESSER	**Nín ne, fūrén?**	And for you, Madame?
MARY	**Wǒ xiǎng xǐfà hé dìngxíng, ránhòu xiūxiuzhījia.**	I'd like a shampoo, and a set, and a manicure.
HAIRDRESSER	**Hǎode. Nín yào rǎnfà ma?**	All right. Would you like a color rinse?
MARY	**Bù. Jīntiān bù. Qǐng búyào yòng fàjiāo.**	No. Not today. And no hairspray, please.
HAIRDRESSER	**Hǎode. Xiànzài nín kéyǐ yòng hōngfàzhào le.**	OK. Now you are ready for the hair dryer.

(After Mary is finished.)

| HAIRDRESSER | **Xiànzài nín zhàozhao jìngzi.** | Now look in the mirror. |
| MARY | **Hěnhǎo. Xièxie.** | Marvelous. Thank you. |

Here are some useful expressions for the beauty parlor. Repeat them aloud as you write them out.

Wǒ xiǎng míngtiān lái lǐfà.	I'd like an appointment for tomorrow.
Nǐ kéyǐ chuīgān wǒde tóufa ma?	Could you blow dry my hair?
Nǐ kéyǐ xǐxi hé jiǎnjian wǒde tóufa ma?	Could you wash and cut my hair?
Wǒ xūyào rǎnfà.	I need a color rinse.

Qǐng jiǎn duǎn yìdiǎnr.	A little shorter, please.
Qǐng jiù ràng tā cháng yìdiǎnr.	Leave it long, please.
Shāowēi yòng yìdiǎnr fàjiāo.	Just a little hairspray.

FOR WOMEN ONLY: You are off to the beauty salon. Do you know what you want? M‍
a list in Chinese just in case.

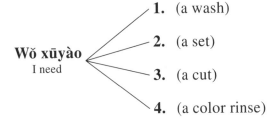

Wǒ xūyào
I need

1. (a wash) _____
2. (a set) _____
3. (a cut) _____
4. (a color rinse) _____

Lǐfàdiàn
Barber Shop

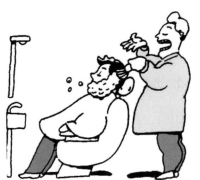

lǐfàyuán
barber

tìguā/guāhúzi
shave

tìxūdāo
razor

zìjǐ guāhúzi
shave oneself

ANSWERS

Beauty salon 1. xǐfà 2. dìngxíng 3. jiǎnfà 4. rǎnfà

Húzi hé Bìnjiǎo

Beard and Sideburns

xiǎohúzi

mustache

shūtóu

to comb/brush

jiǎntóu

cut

zìjǐ shūtóu

to comb/brush one's own hair

Mark needs a haircut. He is at the front desk in the hotel lobby.

MARK	**Nǎlǐ yǒu yìjiā hǎode lǐfàdiàn?**	Where is there a good barber shop?
HOTEL CLERK	**Bīnguǎn jiù yǒu yìjiā.**	There's one in the hotel.
MARK	**Wǒ děi děng hěnjiǔ ma?**	Do I have to wait long?
HOTEL CLERK	**Wǒ xiǎng búhuì ba.**	I don't think so.

(in the barber's)

BARBER	**Nín hǎo. Nín yào lǐ shénme yàngshì de tóufa?**	Hello. How can I help you?
MARK	**Wǒ xiǎng jiǎntóufa hé guāhúzi.**	I want a haircut and a shave.
BARBER	**Nín xiǎng zěnyàng jiǎn?**	How do you want it cut?
MARK	**Hòumiàn jiǎnduǎn, qiánmiàn liú cháng.**	Short in the back, long in the front.

BARBER	**Nín xiǎng xǐ yíxià tóu ma?**	Would you like a shampoo?
MARK	**Duì.**	Yes, please.
BARBER	**Zhè xíng ma?**	Is that all right?
MARK	**Liǎngbiān zài jiǎnduǎn yìdiǎn.**	A little shorter on the sides.
BARBER	**Nín shì zhíjiē wǎng hòu shū ma?**	Do you comb your hair straight back?
MARK	**Búshì. Wǒ shì cóng zuǒbian fenkāi shū.**	No, I have a part on the left.
BARBER	**Nín xiǎng yào diǎn kēlóngxiāngshuǐ ma?**	Would you like some cologne?
MARK	**Hǎode.**	Please.
	Wǒ yào fù duōshǎo qián?	How much do I owe you?

The following expressions will come in handy if you need a haircut and shave in China. In many hotels there is a barber shop, and it can be a pleasant and relaxing half hour out of your busy day. Repeat aloud the important expressions below as you write them out.

Nǎlǐ yǒu yìjiā hǎode lǐfàdiàn?	Where is there a good barber shop?
Wǒ děi děng hěnjiǔ ma?	Do I have to wait long?
Wǒ xiǎng jiǎntóufa.	I would like a haircut.
Wǒ xiǎng guāhúzi.	I would like a shave.
Shàngmiàn shāowēi jiǎn yìdiǎn.	Cut a little off the top.
Qǐng xiūxiu wǒde xiǎohúzi.	Please trim my mustache.
Hòumiàn jiǎnduǎn, qiánmiàn liú cháng.	Short in the back, long in the front.

Wénjùyòngpǐn/Bàngōngshì Yòngpǐn
Stationery Goods/Office Supplies

Zài Bàotan
At the Newsstand

English-language newspapers from overseas and China's Number One English language newspaper *China Daily* are available at the newsstands in major hotels. Some post offices sell newspapers and magazines. And of course, you can also purchase stamps, postcards, envelopes, maps of the city, and some other little things that make fine souvenirs.

zázhì
magazine

bàozhǐ
newspaper

míngxìnpiàn
postcards

yóupiào
stamps

yān
cigarettes

MARY	**Nǐmen yǒu yīngwén bàozhǐ mài ma?**	Do you have newspapers in English?
CLERK	**Yǒu. Wǒmen yǒu «Zhōngguó rìbào» háiyǒu yìxiē qítā de bàozhǐ.**	Yes. We have *China Daily* and some other papers, too.
MARY	**Wǒ xiǎng mǎi zhè jǐzhang míngxìnpiàn.**	I would like to buy these postcards.
CLERK	**Nǐ xūyào yóupiào ma?**	Do you need stamps?
MARY	**Bùxūyào. Wǒ háiyǒu jǐzhāng. Nà shì shénme?**	No. I have some. What are those?

CLERK	**Nà shì yítào shēngrì kǎpiàn. Yítào shí èr zhāng. Měi** zhāng shàngmiàn yǒu yígè bùtóngde dòngwù de huà. Nǐ tīngshuō guò Zhōngguóde shí èr dìzhī ma?	They are a set of birthday cards. Twelve makes a set. Each has a picture of a different animal. Have you heard of the Chinese twelve Earthly Branches?
MARY	**Méiyǒu. Búguò zhè shì bú shì nà shí èr gè dòngwù dàibiǎo shí èr shēngxiāo.**	No. But, are these the twelve animals representing the year in which a person is born?
CLERK	**Duì.**	That's right.
MARY	**Nà tài hǎole. Wǒ yào mǎi yítào.** Duōshǎo qián?	Oh, very good. I'd like to buy one set. How much are they?
CLERK	**Èrshí kuài.**	20 yuan.

Read through the conversation several times and review the new words by doing a matching exercise.

1.	**wénjùyòngpǐn**	a.	birthday cards
2.	**bàotān**	b.	cigarettes
3.	**zázhì**	c.	magazine
4.	**bàozhǐ**	d.	newspaper
5.	**míngxìnpiàn**	e.	newsstand
6.	**yóupiào**	f.	postcards
7.	**yān**	g.	stamps
8.	**shēngrì kǎpiàn**	h.	stationery goods

Zài Wénjùyòngpǐn Diàn

At the Stationery Store

Here are some of the items you might want to purchase at the stationery store. Say them aloud several times.

qiānbǐ
pencil

xìnfēng
envelope

bǐ
pen

tòumíng jiāozhǐ
transparent tape

xiàn
string

bǐjìběn
notebook

xìnjiān
writing pad

xìnzhǐ
writing paper

Read the following passage that Mary wrote about what she did yesterday evening.

Zuótiān wǎnshang wǒ xiǎng gěi yígè péngyou **xiě yìfēng xìn.** Wǒ qù le yìjiā wénjùyòngpǐn diàn. Zài nàr wǒ mǎi le yìběn xìnjiān hé jǐgè xìnfēng. **Wǒ fāxiàn tāmen nàr bú mài yóupiào.** Wǒ děi qù **fùjìn yìjiā yóujú.** Zài nàr wǒ mǎi le jǐzhāng yóupiào hé jǐzhāng míngxìnpiàn. **Zài huílai de lù shàng,** wǒ zài yìjiā kāfēidiàn tíng le yíhuìr, **hē le yìbēi kāfēi.**

Yesterday evening I wanted to write a letter to a friend. I went to the stationery store where I purchased a writing pad and some envelopes. I found out they don't sell stamps there. I had to go to a nearby post office where I bought some stamps and several postcards. On the way home I stopped at a coffee shop and had a cup of coffee.

Choose the correct letter to complete each sentence.

1. **Zuótiān wǎnshang wǒ qù le** _____ .
   a. **yìjiā wénjùyòngpǐn diàn**
   b. **yìjiā yóujú**
   c. **yìjiā kāfēidiàn**
   d. **a, b hé c**

2. **Wǒ zài wénjùyòngpǐndiàn mǎi le** _____ .
   a. **yóupiào**
   b. **jǐzhāng míngxìnpiàn**
   c. **yìběn xìnjiān hé jǐge xìnfēng**
   d. **yìběn xīnjiān**

3. **Wǒ zài yìjiā kāfēidiàn** _____ .
   a. **hē le kāfēi**
   b. **mǎi le yóupiào**
   c. **fā le xìn**
   d. **a, b hé c**

ANSWERS

1.d 2.c 3.a

134

Zhūbǎo Diàn
The Jewelry Store

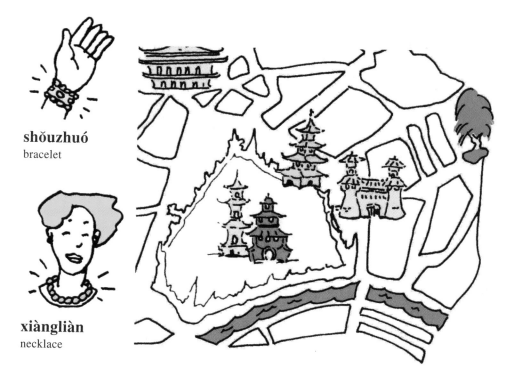

shǒuzhuó
bracelet

xiōngzhēn
brooch

xiàngliàn
necklace

xiàngquān
chain

jièzhi
ring

ěrhuán
earrings

bǎoshí jièzhi
ring with precious stone

Mark goes to a jewelry store to buy a gift for his wife.

SALESCLERK	**Nín xiǎng mǎi yìdiǎn shénme?**	How may I help you?
MARK	**Wǒ xiǎng mǎi yìdiǎn dōngxi gěi wǒde tàitai.**	I would like to buy something for my wife.
SALESCLERK	**Tā xǐhuān shǒuzhuó ma, huòxǔ xǐhuān yín jièzhi?**	Does she like bracelets, or perhaps silver rings?

135

MARK	Bù. Tā gèngxǐhuān jīn de.	No. She prefers gold.
SALESCLERK	Nín juéde zhège xiōngzhēn zěnmeyàng?	How do you like this brooch?
MARK	Hěn piàoliang. Nà yíduì hǔpò ěrhuán yě hěn hǎokàn.	It's beautiful. And those amber earrings are lovely too.
SALESCLERK	Duì. Wǒmen háiyǒu hé zhè xiāngpèide xiàngliàn.	Yes. And we have a matching necklace.
MARK	Shì ma? Yìqi zǒnggòng duōshǎo qián?	You do? How much do they cost together?
SALESCLERK	Liǎng qiān yuán.	Two thousand *yuan*.
MARK	Liǎng qiān yuán! Nǐ yǐwéi wǒ shì ge fù Měiguórén ma?	Two thousand *yuan*! Do you think that I am a rich American?
SALESCLERK	Kě nín yě kěndìng búshì yíge qióng Měiguórén!	But, you are certainly not a poor American, either!
MARK	Jìrán shì zhèyàng, wǒ jiù mǎixià ba. Zhè yítào díquè hěn měi.	In that case, I'll take them. They are indeed a pretty set.
SALESCLERK	Kěndìng nínde tàitai huì xǐhuān de.	I'm sure your wife will love them.

Some of your relatives back home have expensive tastes and want you to bring them a piece of jewelry from China. Can you make out your list in Chinese?

1. Aunt Dottie would like a brooch. ————————————

2. Grandma wants some earrings. ————————————

3. Your daughter-in-law wants a ring. ————————————

4. Grandpa wants a bracelet for his new girlfriend. ————————————

5. Your niece wants an amber necklace. ————————————

Bǎoshí

Precious Stones

Pronounce the words below aloud and write them out in the spaces provided.

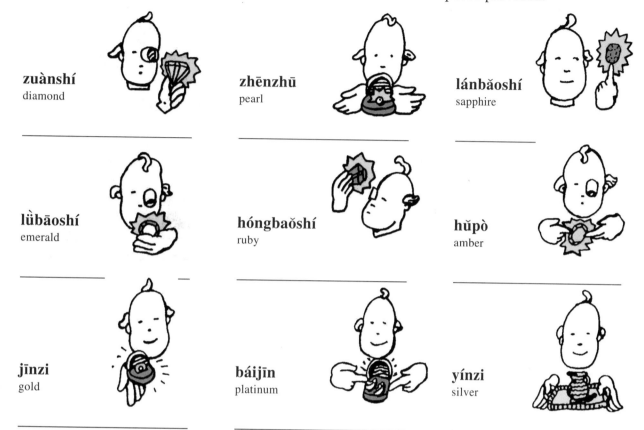

zuànshí
diamond

zhēnzhū
pearl

lánbǎoshí
sapphire

lǜbāoshí
emerald

hóngbaǒshí
ruby

hǔpò
amber

jīnzi
gold

báijīn
platinum

yínzi
silver

Do you remember the adjectives for colors in Chinese? See if you can match the following color adjectives with the names of the precious stones that they modify.

Let's take a quick look at the color words:

lán — blue　　　　**lǜ** — green　　　　**hóng** — red
huáng — yellow　　**bái** — white　　　**hēi** — black

1. **lánbǎoshí**　　　　a. **bái**

2. **lǜbǎoshí**　　　　 b. **hóng**

3. **hóngbǎoshí**　　　 c. **huáng**

4. **jīnzi**　　　　　　 d. **lán**

5. **yínzi**　　　　　　 e. **lǜ**

137

Zhōng/Biǎo

Clocks/Watches

nàozhōng
alarm clock

shóubiǎo
wristwatch

huáibiǎo
pocket watch

zhōngbiǎodiàn
watch repair shop

Practice saying aloud and writing the words from the sentences below. Read them over again until you feel comfortable with the expressions you will need to get your watch repaired.

Can you repair this watch?
Nǐ néng xiūlǐ zhè kuài biǎo ma?

Can you clean my watch?
Nǐ néng qīngxǐ wode biǎo ma?

My watch is fast.
Wǒde biǎo kuài le.

My watch is slow.
Wǒde biǎo màn le.

My watch has stopped running.
Wǒde biǎo tíng le.

My watch doesn't run well.
Wǒde biǎo zǒu de bù zhǔn.

I can't wind it.
Wǒde biǎo bù néng shàng le.

Can you put in a new battery for me?
Nǐ néng wèi wǒ zhuāng shàng xīn diànchí ma?

Yīnwèi (because) . . ., suǒyǐ (so) . . .

In English we do not use both "because" and "so" in one sentence. Chinese do use these two words **yīnwèi** (because) . . ., **suǒyǐ** (so) . . . in the same sentence.

Yīnwèi jīntiān tiānqì bùhǎo, suǒyǐ wǒmen méi qù jiāoyóu.
Because the weather is not good, (so) we did not go on an outing.

Yīnwèi Mǎkè de biǎo huài le, suǒyǐ tā xiǎng mǎi yíkuài xīn biǎo.
Because Mark's watch doesn't work, (so) he wants to buy a new one.

Here are some good reasons for the each of the following sentences. Write them in their proper places.

Yīnwèi tāde biǎo zǒngshì màn, (Because his watch was always slow,)
Yīnwèi wǒde biǎo kuài le, (Because my watch is fast,)
Yīnwèi wǒde biǎo màn le, (Because my watch is slow,)
Yīnwèi wǒde biǎo méi diànchí le, (Because the battery in my watch is dead,)

1. _____ **suǒyǐ wǒ zǎo dào le.**
(I arrived early.)

2. _____ **suǒyǐ wǒ wǎn dào le.**
(I am late.)

3. _____ **suǒyǐ tā tíng le.**
(it stopped.)

4. _____ **suǒyǐ tā yào bǎ biǎo sòngqù qīngxǐ.**
(he had it cleaned.)

lípǐn
gift

píngfēng
folding screen

qīqì
lacquerware

jiǎnzhǐ
paper cut

huāpíng
vase

kuàizi
chopsticks

chájù
tea set

shànzi
fan

xì cíqì
fine china

Make sure you visit the gift shop before you leave. Read carefully how Mark goes shopping for his friends and family back home.

MARK	**Wǒ xiǎng mǎi yìdiǎn jìniànpǐn.**	I would like to purchase some souvenirs.
CLERK	**Nǐ xūyào zhēnzhèngde Zhōngguó jìniànpǐn.**	You need real Chinese souvenirs.
MARK	**Duì. Xiàng sīchóu, huòzhe shì cíqì.**	Yes, like silk, or porcelain.
CLERK	**Wǒmen yǒu hěn hǎokànde shǒujuàn hé tóujīn. Wǒmen yǒu hěn hǎo de xì cí chájù.**	We have lovely handkerchiefs and head scarves. We have very good tea sets made of fine china.

MARK	Zhè tiáo sījīn duōshǎo qián?	How much does this silk scarf cost?
CLERK	Zhè shì zhēnsī de. Zhè yào yì bǎi yuán.	It is real silk. It is 100 yuan.
MARK	Zhè ge qīqì hézi hěn piàoliang. Wǒ xiǎng mǎi yíge. Zhè yíge duōshǎo qián?	This lacquer box is pretty. I'd like to buy one. How much is it?
CLERK	Èr shí kuài. Jǐnguǎn búsuàn piányi, kě yě búsuàn tài guì.	20 yuan. Although it is not cheap, it is not too expensive, either.
MARK	Nǐmen shōu xìnyòng kǎ ma?	Do you take a credit card?
CLERK	Wǒmen shōu.	Yes, we do.

Read the following statements and write in the answer **Duì** (True) or **Búduì** (False) according to the dialogue.

1. Mǎkè xiǎng mǎi yìdiǎn zhēnzhèngde Zhōngguó jìniànpǐn. _____

2. Nà tiáo sījīn shì zhēnsi de. _____

3. Mǎkè mǎi le yíge qiqì hézi. Nàge qiqì hézi hěn piàoliang. _____

4. Nà tiáo tóujīn yào èr shí kuài qián. _____

5. Nàjia lǐpǐndiàn bùshōu xìnyòng kǎ. _____

Chàngpiàn Shāngdiàn
The Record Store

héshì lùyīncídài
cassette tape

jīguāng chàngpán
CD (compact disc)

chàngpiàn
record

lùxiàngdài
videocassette

mínjiān yīnyuè
folk music

gǔdiǎn yīnyuè
classical music

liúxíng yīnyuè
pop music

shōuyīnjī
radio

diànshìjī
television

liúshēngjī
record player
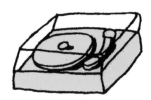

lùyīnjī
tape recorder

lùxiàngjī
VCR (videocassette recorder)

màikèfēng
microphone

Try to read aloud the following paragraph about listening to music.

Māma hé bàba fēicháng xǐhuān yīnyuè.

Zài Běijīng de shíhòu, Tāmen

qù le chàngpiàn shāngdiàn.

Zài nàr māma mǎi le jǐzhāng qīngyīnyuè

de chàngpiàn. Yīnwèi tā hěn xǐhuān

qīngyīnyuè. Ta yǒu yígè liúshēngjī.

Bàba fēicháng xǐhuān Zhōngguó mínjiān

yīnyuè. Tā mǎi le jǐhé héshì lùyīncídài.

Tā yǒu yígè lùyīnjī. Xiànzài zài wǒmen

jiā nǐ suíshí dōu kéyǐ tīng

Zhōngguó yīnyuè le.

Mom and Dad like music very much.

When they were in Beijing, they

went to a record store.

There Mom bought several records of

light music because she likes light music

very much. She has a record player.

Dad likes Chinese folk music,

and he bought some cassette tapes.

He has a tape recorder. Now in our

house you can listen

to Chinese music at any time.

Read over the paragraph one more time and then try to write out the missing words in the blanks.

1. Māma hé bàba _____ xǐhuān yīnyuè.
   (very much)

2. Māma mǎi le jǐzhāng _____ de chàngpiàn.
   (light music)

3. Bàba fēicháng xǐhuān _____ .
   (Chinese folk music)

4. Tā mǎi le jǐhé _____ .
   (cassette tapes)

5. Xiànzài zài wǒmen jiā nǐ _____ dōu kéyǐ tīng Zhōngguó yīnyuè le.
   (at any time)

Zhàoxiàng Qìcái

Photographic Supplies

yìnxiàng
to print

zhàoxiàngjī
camera

diànchí
battery

huàndēngpiàn
slides

jiāojuǎn
film

shèxiàngjī
video camera

At the photo counter Mary tries to get her slides developed and also buy some film.

MARY	**Nǐmen zhèr chōngxǐ huàndēngpiàn ma?**	Do you develop slides here?
CLERK	**Wǒmen chōngxǐ. Qǐng nín tián hǎo zhège.**	Yes, we do. If you will fill this out.
MARY	**Hǎode. Shénme shíhòu néng chōngxǐ hǎo?**	All right. When will this be ready?
CLERK	**Xīngqī wǔ néng chōngxǐ hǎo.**	It will be ready on Friday.
MARY	**Wǒ xiǎng mǎi liǎng juǎn 135 háomǐ de cǎisè jiāojuǎn, yào 24 zhāng de. Wǒde shǎnguāngdēng hái xūyào sì ge diànchí.**	And I'd like two rolls of 135 millimeter color film with 24 exposures. And I need four batteries for my flash.

Look at the following pictures and write their names in the spaces provided.

1. 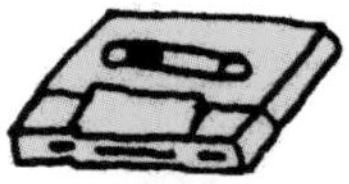 ______________________

2. 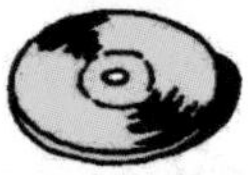 ______________________

3. 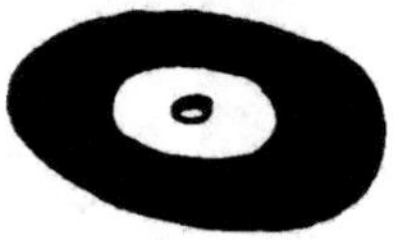 ______________________

4. 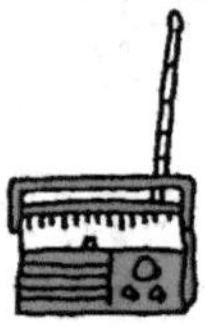 ______________________

5. 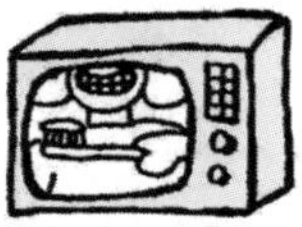 ______________________

6. 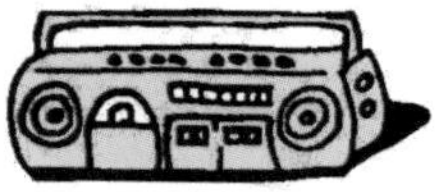 ______________________

7. 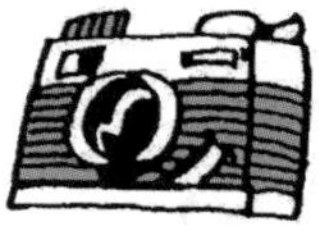 ______________________

8. 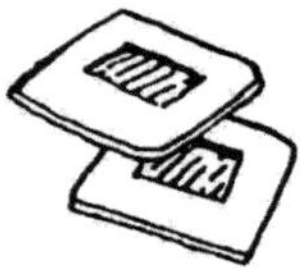 ______________________

9. 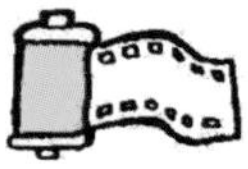 ______________________

10. 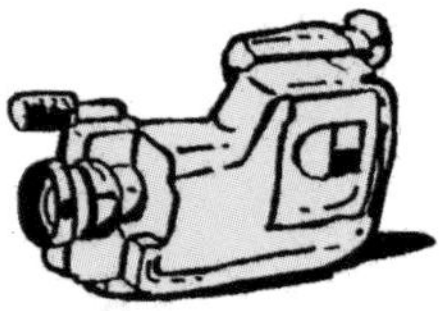 ______________________

ANSWERS

1. héshì lùyīncídài **2.** jīguāng chàngpán **3.** chàngpiàn **4.** shōuyīnjī **5.** diànshìjī
6. lùyīnjī **7.** zhàoxiàngjī **8.** huàndēngpiàn **9.** jiāojuǎn **10.** shèxiàngjī

yǎnjìngshāng
optician

yǎnjìng
glasses

yǎnjìngjià
frame

**yǐnxíng
yǎnjìngpiàn**
contact lenses

Yǎnjìngshāng
Optician

Read the following dialogue at the optician's.

MARK	**Wǒde yǎnjìngjià hé yǎnjìngpiàn huàile. Nǐ néng xiūhǎo ma?**	The frame and a lens of my glasses are broken. Can you fix them?
OPTICIAN	**Nín yǒu yífù bèiyòngde yǎnjìng ma?**	Do you have a spare pair?

146

MARK	Wǒ méi yǒu.	No, I don't.
OPTICIAN	Jìrán shì zhèyàng, wǒ jìnkuài de wèi nín xiūhǎo.	In that case, I will fix them for you as soon as possible.
	Liǎng xiǎoshí hòu lái qǔ.	Come back in two hours.
	Wǒ bāng nín xiūhǎo.	I'll have them ready for you.
MARK	Zhēn tài gǎnxiè le.	I am grateful.

Xiézi Xiūlǐ
Shoe Repairs

xiédài
shoelace

xiédiàn
insole

xiézi
shoes

All around town you are likely to see tiny shoeshine and shoe repair booths. At the booths you can have minor repairs performed. For major repairs you can bring your shoes or boots to the shoe repair shops.

MARY	Nǐ kéyǐ xiūlǐ wǒde xiézi ma?	Can you repair my shoes?
COBBLER	Nǎlǐ huàile?	What's wrong?
MARY	Xiégēn.	The heels.
COBBLER	Qǐng zuòxià lai bǎ xié tuōxià lai.	If you will take that seat and take your shoes off…
MARY	Nǐ xiànzài jiù kéyǐ xiū?	You can do them now?
	Nà tài hǎole.	That's good.

Go over the material for the optician and shoe repair shops. Then see if you can fill in the blanks provided for the following emergency situations.

1. You have broken your eyeglasses. Ask if they can be repaired.

   Nǐ néng xiūhǎo wǒde _____ **ma?**

2. Explain that you have broken a lens and the frame.

   Wǒde yǎnjìngjià hé yǎnjìngpiàn _____ .

3. Tell your optician that you don't have a spare pair of glasses.

   Wǒ _____ **yífù bèiyòngde yǎnjìng.**

4. You have broken your heel. Tell the shoemaker what you need.

   Nǐ kéyǐ xiūlǐ wǒde _____ **ma?**

25	Yínháng
	Bank

Rénmínbì

Currency

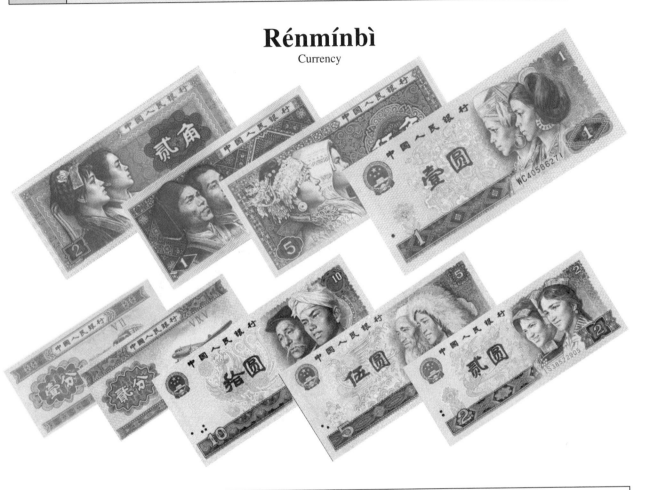

The official name for the currency of China is **Rénmínbì** (RMB—the "people's money"). It is denominated into the **yuán,** which is also counted out as **kuài.** Notes in common use are printed in denominations of 1, 2, 5, 10, 50, and 100 **yuán.** The smallest unit is **fen.**

1 **yuán** = 10 **máo/jiǎo** = 100 **fēn**

1 **máo/jiǎo** = 10 **fēn**

Coins are in denominations of 1 **fēn,** 2 **fēn,** 5 **fēn,** 1 **máo/jiǎo,** 2 **máo/jiǎo,** 5 **máo/jiǎo,** and 1 **yuán.**

As you repeat aloud the following denominations of bills and coins, notice that the form of the word is determined by the number.

Zhǐbì		
Bank Notes		
1 fēn	1 jiǎo	1 yuán
2 fēn	2 jiǎo	2 yuán
5 fēn	5 jiǎo	5 yuán
		10 yuán
		50 yuán
		100 yuán

Yìngbì		
Coins		
1 fēn	1 jiǎo	1 yuán
2 fēn	2 jiǎo	
5 fēn	5 jiǎo	

Rén hé Wù

People and Things

qián
money

yínháng
bank

xiànjīn
cash

yìngtōnghuòbì

hard currency

jīnglǐ

manager

**chūnàyuán
chuāngkǒu**

teller's window

lǚxíng zhīpiào

travelers' checks

zhànghù

account

dàikuǎn

loan

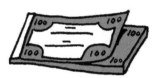

cúnkuǎndān

deposit slip

xìnyòng kǎ

credit card

qǔkuǎndān

withdrawal slip

Zěnyàng

How To

duìhuàn

exchange

duìhuàn lǜ

rate of exchange

fùzhàng

pay

kāihù

open an account

cún kuǎn/qián

make a deposit

qǔ kuǎn/qián

make a withdrawal

qiānmíng/qiānzì

sign

Rénmínbì is the only money that is used in China. So you need to exchange your U.S. dollars into **Rénmínbì.** You can exchange your money at the Bank of China, whose branches are located at the major airports, hotels, and city areas. To exchange money in China, you need to show your passport.

Mark Smith is at the bank located in his hotel. He needs to exchange some money.

| MARK | **Wǒ xiǎng bǎ zhèzhāng 100 kuài qián de Měijīn lǚxíng zhīpiào duìhuàn chéng Rénmínbì.** | I want to exchange this $100 American traveler's check for Renminbi. |
| TELLER | **Hǎode. Qǐng zài zhīpiào shàng qiānzì. Wǒ xūyào kàn nínde hùzhào.** | All right. Please sign the check. And I need to see your passport. |

MARK	Hǎode. Zhè shì wǒde hùzhào.	OK. Here is my passport.
TELLER	Xièxie.	Thank you.
	Nín shì xiǎng yào dà piàomiàn de	Would you like the Renminbi
	háishì xiǎo piàomiànde Rénmínbì?	in large bills or small ones?
MARK	Qǐng gěi wǒ xiǎo piàomiànde.	Small bills, please.
TELLER	Shǐmìsī Xiānsheng,	Mr. Smith, here is your money
	zhèshì nínde qián hé hùzhào.	and your passport.
MARK	Xièxie.	Thank you.
TELLER	Zàijiàn.	Good-bye.

Now look at the pictures and say the words aloud. Then write them in the blanks provided.

1. _____

2. _____

3. _____

4. _____

5. _____

6. _____

shì . . . de

Like the English sentence structure "It is . . . that(who)," Chinese has the **shì . . . de** pattern to emphasize the time, place, manner or some other detail of a completed action.

Example: **Tā zuótiān dào Běijīng.**   He arrived in Beijing yesterday.
Tā shì zuótiān dào Běijīng de.   It was yesterday that he arrived in Beijing.

Wǒ chéng fēijī qù.   I went by plane.
Wǒ shì chéng fēijī qù de.   It was by plane that I went.

In the negative sentence, use **búshì . . . de**

Tā búshì zuótiān dào Běijīng de.   It was not yesterday morning that he came.
Wǒ búshì chéng fēijī qù de.   It was not by plane that I went.

Now try to emphasize the following sentences by adding **shì . . . de** in the proper places.

1. Where did she exchange her money?   (at the bank at the airport)
Tā zài jīchǎng yínháng duìhuàn.

_____

2. Where did Mark exchange his money?   (at the bank in his hotel)
Tā zài bīnguǎn yínháng duìhuàn.

_____

3. Where did Mary buy some stamps?   (at the post office)
Tā zài yóujú mǎi.

_____

4. How did they go to the Great Wall?   (by taxi)
Tāmen chéng chūzūqìchē qù.

_____

Most post offices handle domestic telegrams and long-distance telephone services as well as mail service. Major hotels also provide these services.

Read the following story about our amateur postman. Some of the words you will need are on the following pages.

Fāngfang hé tāde xiǎo érzi, Bōbo zài tánhuà.

Fangfang is speaking with Bobo, her little son.

—Bōbo, **nǐ yídà zǎo zài gàn shénme?**

"Bobo, what are you doing so early?"

—Wǒ zài zhuāng yóudìyuán.

"I'm playing mailman."

—Yóudìyuán. Nǐde xìn ne?

"Mailman. Where are your letters?"

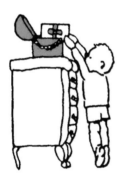

—Māma, wǒ yǒu xìn.

"I have letters, Mom."

—Nǐ nǎrlái de xìn?

"Where from?"

—**Wǒ shì cóng nǐde bìchú lǐ ná de.**

"I got them from your closet."

—Shì nàxiē jìzhe fěnhóng cǎidàide xìnfēng ma?

"Those envelopes with the pink ribbon?"

—Shìde māma. **Wǒ gāng bǎ tāmen fēnfā gěi línjū.**

"Yes, Mom. I gave them out to the neighbors."

—**Tiān'a.** Nà shì bàba xiě de qíngshū.

"My goodness. Those are the love letters from Papa!"

yóuxiāng
mailbox

diànbào
telegram

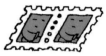

yóupiào
stamps

xìn
letter

míngxìnpiàn
postcard

yóudìyuán
mailman

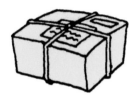

bāoguǒ
package

Mark discusses the mail service with the hotel clerk.

MARK	**Wǒ xiǎng jì yìfēng**	I want to send an airmail
	hángkōng xìn dào Měiguó.	letter to the USA.
	Wǒ kéyǐ zài nǎr jì?	Where can I do this?
CLERK	**Nín rúguǒ yǒu yóupiào, nín**	If you have a stamp, you
	kéyǐ bǎ xìn tóujìn jiē shàng	can put your letter in any
	rènhé yíge yóuxiāng lǐ.	mailbox on the street.

MARK	**Wǒ yě xǔyào jì zhè ge bāoguǒ.**	I also need to mail this package.
CLERK	**Nàme nín jiùděi qù yóujú le.**	Then you have to go to the post office.
MARK	**Wǒ kéyǐ zài nǎr fā diànbào huò fā chuánzhēn ne?**	Where can I send a telegram or fax?
CLERK	**Yě zài yóujú. Nín hái kéyǐ zài nàr dǎ chángtú diànhuà.**	Also at the post office. You can also place your long-distance phone calls there.
MARK	**Hǎoxiàng zài yóujú wǒ kéyǐ gàn suǒyǒude shìqing.**	It seems that I can almost do everything at the post the office.
CLERK	**Nín shuō de duì. Nín hái kéyǐ zài yóujú mǎi bàozhǐ hé zázhì.**	You are right. You can also buy some newspapers and magazines from the post office.
MARK	**Zhè hěn yǒuqù. Wǒ zhēn děi qù kànkan.**	That's interesting. I really should go and see then.

Zài Yóujú

At the Post Office

MARK — **Wǒ yào jì yìfēng hěn zhòngyàode xìn dào Měiguó.** — I want to send an important letter to the USA.

POSTAL CLERK — **Nín kéyǐ jì hángkōng xìn, bìngqiě guàhào.** — It can be sent via airmail, and as a registered letter.

MARK — **Wǒ yě xūyào jì zhè ge bāoguǒ. Yóufèi shì duōshǎo?** — I need to send this package, too. How much is the postage?

POSTAL CLERK — **Wǒ xūyào chēng yi chēng nínde bāoguǒ cái zhīdao. Bāoguǒ jì hángkōng shì 25 yuán, xìn shì 3 yuán.** — I need to weigh your package to find out. 25 yuan for the package by airmail, 3 yuan for your letter.

MARK — **Xièxie.** — Thank you.

Fill in the Chinese expression for each picture.

1. _____

2. _____

3. _____

4. _____

5. _____

6. _____

7. _____

Wèi! Wèi!
Hello! Hello!

You can usually place local calls from your hotel room, either by dialing directly or by dialing a single number for an outside line. For international calls you may have to place an order through the international operator.

Here are some useful expressions for making telephone calls in China.

Wǒ kéyǐ jièyòng yíxià nǐde diànhuà ma?   Can I use your phone?

Nǐde diànhuà hàomǎ shì duōshǎo?   What is your telephone number?

Dìqūhào shì duōshǎo?   And the area code?

Jiēxiànyuán, wǒ xiǎng dǎ yíge _____ .   Operator, I want to place a (an) _____ .

chángtú diànhuà   long-distance call

guójì chángtú diànhuà   international call

duìfāng fùkuǎnde diànhuà   collect call

Jiēxiànyuán, qǐng nǐ bāng wǒ bō zhè ge hàomǎ.
Operator, would you please dial this number for me?

159

Wǒ jiǎnzhí tīngbújiàn.
I can barely hear you.

Diànhuà zhànxiàn.
The line is busy.

Wèi, wǒ shì Mǎlì.
Hello, this is Mary.

gōngyòng diànhuà
pay telephone

náqǐ diànhuàtǒng
lift the receiver

Wǒde diànhuàxiàn duànle.
I've been disconnected.

Bié guà diànhuà!
Don't hang up!

Wèi, Mǎkè zài ma?
Hello, may I speak to Mark?

diànhuà bù
telephone book

bō hào
dial a number

Zài Diànhuà Tíng
At the Telephone Booth

| MARK | **Hǎode. (duì zìjǐ) Shǒuxiān wǒ náqǐ diànhuàtǒng, ránhòu, tóujìn yìngbì. Děngzhe bōhàoyīn, ránhòu, bōhào. Wèi! Wèi! Wáng Gāng zài ma?** | Yes. (to himself) First I lift the receiver, then I put in the coins. Wait for the dial tone, and then dial the number. Hello! Hello! May I speak to Wang Gang, please? |
| A VOICE | **Wǒ jiǎnzhí tīng bújiàn. Qǐng dà diǎn shēng shuōhuà.** | I can barely hear you. Please speak louder. |

MARK	Wǒ zhǎo Wáng Gāng.	I'd like to speak to Wang Gang.
A VOICE	Nǐ bō cuò hào le.	You have the wrong number.
MARK	Duìbuqǐ.	Sorry.
	(Tā fàngxià diànhuàtǒng huí bīnguǎn le.)	(He puts down the receiver and goes back to his hotel.)

Match the following sentences with the English equivalents.

1. Wǒ kéyǐ jièyòng yíxià nǐde diànhuà ma?   a. What's the area code?

2. Nǐde diànhuà hàomǎ shì duōshǎo?   b. Can I use your phone?

3. Dìqūhào shì duōshǎo?   c. I've been disconnected.

4. Wǒ xiǎng dǎ duìfāng fùkuǎnde diànhuà.   d. I can barely hear you.

5. Wǒ jiǎnzhí tīng bújiàn.   e. I want to place a collect call.

6. Wǒde diànhuàxiàn duànle.   f. The line is busy.

7. Diànhuà zhànxiàn.   g. What is your telephone number?

8. Nǐ bō cuò hào le.   h. You have the wrong number.

Cóng Tóu Dào Jiǎo

From Head to Toe

Mark and Mary are studying the parts of the body. See if you can learn the words along with them.

MARK   **Hǎo, shuí xiān kāishǐ,**   Well, who should begin—

         shì nǐ hái shì wǒ?   you or I?

MARY   **Nǐ xiān wèn wǒ.**   You ask me first

MARK   **Hǎode. Zhè shì shénme?**   Okay, what's this?

MARY   **Tóufa.**   Hair.

MARK   **Zhè shì shénme?**   And what is this?

MARY   **Yǎnjīng.**   Eyes.

MARK   **Yǎnjīng zhōngjiān ne?**   And between the eyes?

MARY   **Bízi.**   Nose.

         Hǎo, gāi wǒ wèn nǐ le.   OK. My turn.

         Zhè shì nǐde zuǐba,   This is your mouth,

         zuǐba shàngmiàn   but what is above

         shì shénme?   the mouth?

MARK	Nǐ shì zhǐ wǒde xiǎohúzi ma?		Do you mean my mustache?
MARY	Shì. Nǐ yǒu yìzhī ěrduō ma?		Yes. Do you have one ear?
MARK	Búduì. Liǎngzhī ěrduō hé liǎngge yǎnjīng.		No, two ears and two eyes.
MARY	Zhè shì wǒde liǎnjiá.		And this is my cheek.
MARK	Zhè shì nǐde liǎn		And this is your face,
	hé tóu.		and your head.
MARY	Nǐ xiào de shíhòu, wǒ kàn jiàn . . .		When you smile, I see . . .
MARK	Wǒde yáchǐ. Zài yīshēng nàr wǒ shēnchū . . .		My teeth. At the doctor's I put out my . . .
MARY	Shétou.		tongue.
	Zhè shì xiàba.		This is the chin.

163

MARK	**Zhè dāngrán shì bózi.**		And this is, of course, the neck.
MARY	**Zhè shì jiānbǎng.**		Here are shoulders.
MARK	**Yìzhī gēbo, liǎngzhi gēbo . . .**		One arm, two arms . . .
MARY	**Zhè shì wǒde zhǒu.**		This is my elbow.
MARK	**Nǐ yǒu jǐge zhítou?**		How many fingers do you have?
MARY	**Wǒ yǒu shí ge zhítou.**		I have ten fingers.
MARK	**Xiànzài yòu lún dào wǒ le. Zhè shì bèi. Qiánmiàn shì . . .**		Now my turn again. This is the back. In front is the . . .
MARY	**Xiōng.**		chest.
MARK	**Nǐ chī tài duō de shíhòu, shénme dìfāng tòng?**		When you eat too much, what hurts?
MARY	**Wǒde wèi.**		My stomach.

MARK	**Duì. Wèi yǐxià de bùwèi shì . . .**	That's correct. And under the stomach we find . . .
MARY	**Dùzi.**	the belly.
MARK	**Hòumiàn shì . . .**	And in the back is the . . .
MARY	**Túnbù.**	backside.
MARK	**Nǐ yǒu yíge xīgài ma?**	And do you have one knee?
MARY	**Búduì. Wǒ yǒu liǎng ge xīgài.**	No. I have two knees.
MARK	**Liǎng tiáo tuǐ.**	And two legs.
MARY	**Měi zhī jiǎo yǒu jiǎodǐ, jiǎogēn hé . . .**	And each foot has a sole, heel, and...
MARK	**Wǔ ge jiǎozhítou.**	five toes.

That was certainly a lot of new words to learn. Try repeating them to yourself several times and then see if you can draw lines matching the Chinese words with their English equivalents.

1. tuǐ/jiǎo	a. arm
2. ěrduō	b. belly
3. zhǒu	c. ear
4. zhítou	d. elbow
5. gēbo	e. finger
6. tóu	f. head
7. zuǐba	g. knee
8. xīgài	h. leg/foot
9. jiānbǎng	i. mouth
10. dùzi	j. shoulder

fèi
lung

xīnzàng
heart

gānzàng
liver

wèi
stomach

jīròu
muscle

chángzi
intestines

dòngmài
artery

shènzàng
kidney

jìngmài
vein

Nǐ Nǎli Bù Shūfu?

What's Wrong with You?

To tell what's wrong with you in Chinese, you can say
Wǒ huàn (I'm suffering from) + a symptom.
or simply say
Wǒ + the symptom (**le**).

ANSWERS

Matching 1. h 2. c 3. d 4. e 5. a 6. f 7. i 8. g 9. j 10. b

166

Practice saying the following expressions. They might come in handy in case you have to go to a doctor.

Wǒ (huàn) gǎnmào le. I have a cold.

Wǒ biànbì le. I have constipation. (I am constipated.)

Wǒ késou le. I have a cough.

Wǒ (huàn) fùxiè. I have diarrhea.

Wǒ fāshāo le. I have a fever.

Wǒ tóutòng. I have a headache.

Wǒ ěxīn. I have nausea. (I am nauseated.)

Wǒ huàn liúgǎn le. I have the flu.

Wǒ yátòng. I have a toothache.

Wǒ wèitòng. I have an upset stomach.

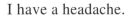
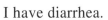

Qǐng Shuō "A"

Say "Aaah," Please

If you need to see a doctor or a dentist while in China, your hotel staff can probably recommend one who speaks English. Still, it's a good idea to learn some of the expressions in these dialogues.

Mark has a sore throat. He has an appointment with Dr. Wang, a general practitioner.

DR. WANG	Shǐmìsī Xiānsheng?	Mr. Smith?
	Wǒ shì Wáng dàifu.	I'm Dr. Wang.
	Nǐ nǎli bù shūfu?	What seems to be the matter?
MARK	Wǒde hóulóng hěn tòng.	My throat is very sore.
DR. WANG	Qǐng bǎ zuǐ zhāngkāi.	Open your mouth, please.
	Shuō "A." Shìde, nǐde	Say "Aah." Yes, your
	hóulóng hóng de hěn	throat is quite red.
	lìhai. Háiyǒu qítāde	Are there any other
	zhèngzhuàng ma?	symptoms?
MARK	Wǒde tóu hěn tòng érqiě	My head aches and
	wǒ gǎndào hěn lèi.	I'm very tired.
DR. WANG	Nǐ fāshāo ma?	Any fever?
MARK	Yǒu yìdiǎn.	Yes.
DR. WANG	Zhè shì nǐde chǔfāng.	Here's a prescription for
	Zhè ge yào yìtiān chī	you. Take the medicine
	sān cì.	three times a day.
	Rúguǒ liǎng sān tiān hòu	If you don't feel better
	bú jiàn hǎozhuǎn, wǒ zài	in two or three days, I will
	gěi nǐ yíge chǔfāng.	change the prescription
		for you.
MARK	Xièxie.	Thank you.

Yáyī: Bǎ Zuǐ Zhāngkāi

The Dentist: Open Your Mouth

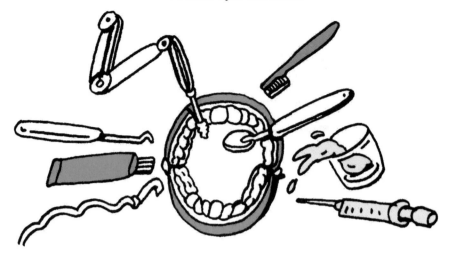

It's not an enjoyable time when you have to go to a dentist. Let's see how Mary does at the local dentist's.

MARY	**Wǒde yá tòng de hěn lìhai.**	I have a terrible toothache.
DENTIST	**Nǐ néng gàosu wǒ nǎli tòng ma?**	Can you show me where it hurts?
MARY	**Wǒ xiǎng shì zhè kē yá.**	It's this tooth, I think.
DENTIST	**Nǐ bǔ yá de dōngxī diàole.**	You've lost a filling.
MARY	**Nà zěnme bàn ne?**	What can you do about it?
DENTIST	**Rúguǒ nǐ yuànyì de huà, wǒ xiànzài kéyǐ gěi nǐ zànshí bǔ shàng. Děng nǐ huí qù hòu, zài zhǎo zìjǐde yáyī.**	If you like, now I can give you a temporary filling. And when you go back home, you can see your own dentist.
MARY	**Nà hǎo. Jiù zhème bàn.**	That's good. Go ahead.
DENTIST	**Nǐ xiǎng dǎ yíjì júbù mázuì zhēn ma?**	Would you like an injection of local anesthesia?
MARY	**Bù xiǎng da. Kě yòu yǒu shénme bànfǎ ne?**	No. But what can I do?

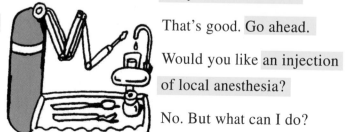

169

Zài Yīyuàn

At the Hospital

Now read along as Mark describes his visit to a Chinese hospital.

Jīntiān zǎoshang wǒ tūrán gǎndào bù shūfu. Tāmen qǐng lái le yīshēng. Yīshēng gěi wǒ zuòle jiǎnchá. Ránhòu tā jiànyì wǒ qù yīyuàn. Zài yīyuàn yíwèi hùshi liángle wǒde xuèyā hé tǐwēn. Ránhòu tāmen zuòle xuèyàng fēnxī. Yīshēng tīngle wǒde màibó, xīnzàng hé fèibù. Tā juédìng bú zuò shǒushù. Yīshēng gěi wǒ dǎ le yì zhēn, kāile yíge chǔfāng yào wǒ chi yào.

This morning I suddenly felt ill. They called in a doctor. The doctor examined me and then suggested that I go to a hospital. At the hospital a nurse took my blood pressure and temperature. Then they did a blood analysis. The doctor took my pulse and listened to my heart and lungs. He decided not to perform an operation, but gave me a shot, and wrote out a prescription for some medicine.

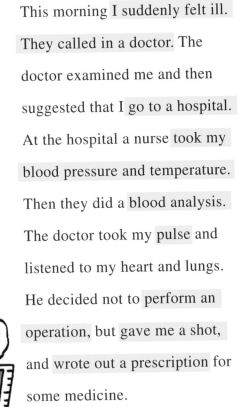

Read the passage above again and try to answer the following questions; write your answers in the spaces provided.

1. **Nàtiān zǎoshang Mǎkè zěnme le?**   What happened to Mark that morning?

   _____

2. **Yīshēng zěnme jiànyì de?**   What did the doctor suggest?

   _____

3. **Zài yīyuàn hùshi duì ta zuòle xiē shénme?**   What did the nurse do to Mark at the
   hospital?

   _____

4. **Yīshēng juédìng gěi tā zuò shǒushù ma?**   Did the doctor decide to do ("give him")
   an operation?

   _____

5. **Yīshēng hòulái zěnme zuòde?**   What did the doctor do instead?

   _____

ANSWERS

1. Nàtiān zǎoshang tā tūrán gǎndào bù shūfu.   2. Yīshēng jiànyì tā qù yīyuàn.   3. Zài yīyuàn yìwèi hùshi liàngle tāde xuěyā hé tǐwēn.   4. Méiyǒu./ Yīshēng juédìng bú zuò shǒushù.   5. Yīshēng gěi tā dǎ le yì zhēn, kāile yìgē chǔfāng.

Jǐnjí Qíngkuàng

An Emergency

China has traditionally been a safe country for tourists, but while most people are honest, friendly, and helpful, hard economic times have given rise to more street crime.

We hope you don't find yourself in a medical or other emergency situation, but it is a good idea to know some useful words and phrases.

First, here are the vital phone numbers:

Huǒjǐng   119
Fire

Jǐngchá   110
Police

Jiùhùchē hé Yīliáo Jíjiù

Ambulance and Medical Help

 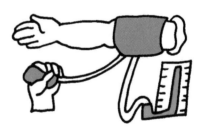

To get emergency medical aid from your hotel, notify the key lady on your floor or the front desk staff. They can call for an ambulance with trained medical personnel to assist you on the spot or to transport you to a hospital. Here are a few expressions for you to learn.

jiùhùchē
ambulance

jǐnjí qíngkuàng
emergency

yīyuàn
hospital

Láirénna!	Help!
Qǐng yīshēng lái!	Call for a doctor!
Jiào jiùhùchē!	Call an ambulance!
Sòng wǒ qù yīyuàn ba!	Take me to a hospital!
Wǒ diēleyìjiāo.	I had a fall.
Wǒ bèi chē zhuàngle.	I was hit by a car.
Wǒde xīnzàngbìng fāzuò le.	I'm having a heart attack.
Wǒ tàngshāng zìjǐ le.	I burned myself.
Wǒ gēshāng zìjǐ le.	I cut myself.
Wǒ zài liúxuè.	I'm bleeding.
Wǒ liúle hěnduō xuè.	I've lost a lot of blood.
Wǒ xiǎng zhè gēn gútou duàn le.	I think the bone is broken.
Zhè tiáo tuǐ zhǒng le.	The leg is swollen.
Zhè ge shǒuwàn niǔshāng le.	The wrist is twisted.
Wǒde jiǎowàn niǔle.	My ankle is dislocated.

Jǐngchá

The Police

jǐngchá
policeman

jǐngchájú
police station

In most cities in China you can find police officers directing traffic and patrolling the streets. If you have problems, the police can probably help you—from finding your way to finding lost items. Items that you have lost often turn up. If you do leave something in a restaurant, a museum or hotel, don't assume it's gone forever. As usual, check first with your hotel front desk staff, or with the police.

Here are some expressions you should know in case you need to call the police.

Jiào jǐngchá!

Call the police!

Jǐngchá jú zài nǎr?

Where is the nearest police station?

Wǒde hùzhào diūle.

I've lost my passport.

Wǒ mílù le.

I'm lost.

Wǒde qiánbāo bèi tōu le.

My wallet has been stolen.

BEFORE YOU LEAVE
Chūfāqián

You've learned a lot of Chinese by now—probably much more than you realize. This section is a very important step in the learning process—a step in which you can review and solidify your understanding of the new language.

The section is organized around basic situations you might encounter. For each situation there are a number of questions about appropriate Chinese expressions. If you have difficulty remembering what to say in a particular situation, review the relevant unit in this book.

Good luck and have a good trip!

Situation 1: Jiéshí Rénmen
Getting to Know People

1. When you meet a Chinese person, how do you start up a conversation?
   a. **Zàijiàn.**
   b. **Nǐ/Nín hǎo.**
   c. **Xièxie.**

2. It is morning and you meet someone. How do you greet him/her?
   a. **Zǎoshang hǎo.**
   b. **Xiàwǔ hǎo.**
   c. **Wǎnshang hǎo.**

3. Someone says **Xièxie.** (Thank you.) to you. How should you reply?
   a. **Xièxie.**
   b. **Nǐ hǎo.**
   c. **Búkèqi.**

4. If a Chinese person says his name is Wang Gang, you call him which of the following?
   a. **Wáng Xiānsheng**
   b. **Gāng Xiānsheng**
   c. **Xiānsheng Wáng**

5. When you want to say hello to an elderly person in China, you should say:
   a. **Nín hǎo.**
   b. **Nǐ hǎo.**
   c. **Nǐ zǎo.**

ANSWERS

Situation 1 1.b 2.a 3.c 4.a 5.a

Situation 2: Dǐdá

Arrival

1. You have a reservation for two rooms at a hotel. What do you say?
   a. **Wǒmen yùdìng le liǎng ge fángjiān.**
   b. **Wǒmen yào liǎng ge fángjiān.**
   c. **Wǒmen yùdìng le yíge fángjiān.**

2. The clerk asks how long you will be staying. Your reply is "About a week."
   a. **Dàyuē yíge yuè.**
   b. **Dàyuē yì tiān.**
   c. **Dàyuē yì xīngqī.**

3. You want to know whether breakfast is included in the price of the room. So you say:
   a. **Fángjià bāokuò wǎncān ma?**
   b. **Fángjià bāokuò zǎocān ma?**
   c. **Fángjià bāokuò zhōngcān ma?**

4. You want to find out where the elevator is.
   a. **Wǒde fángjiān zài nǎr?**
   b. **Diàntī zài nǎr?**
   c. **Kāfēi diàn zài nǎr?**

Situation 3: Guānguāng

Seeing the Sights

1. Suggest to your companion that you go by subway.
   a. **Wǒmen chéng dìtiě ba.**
   b. **Wǒmen dā chūzū qìchē qù ba.**
   c. **Wǒmen chéng gōnggòngqìchē ba.**

2. You are on foot and you want to find a certain museum. You ask someone:
   a. **Qǐngwèn, bówùguǎn hěn dà ma?**
   b. **Qǐngwèn, bówùguǎn hěn yuǎn ma?**
   c. **Qǐngwèn, qù bówùguǎn zěnme zǒu?**

ANSWERS

Situation 2 1. a 2. c 3. b 4. b   Situation 3 1. a 2. c

3. Your watch doesn't work. You want to know the time.
So you ask someone near you:
   a. **Xiànzài jǐ diǎn zhōng?**
   b. **Xiànzài shénme zhōng?**
   c. **Xiànzài jǐ shíjiān?**

4. Can you ask the price of a round-trip ticket to Guangzhou?
   a. **Qù Guǎngzhōu de chēpiào duōshǎo qián?**
   b. **Qù Guǎngzhōu de láihuí chēpiào duōshǎo qián?**
   c. **Qù Guǎngzhōu de láihuí chēpiào hěn guì ma?**

5. You want to know what time your train leaves. You ask:
   a. **Shénme shíjiān kāiche?**
   b. **Shénme shíjiān shàngchē?**
   c. **Shénme shíjiān tíngchē?**

6. Tell your hosts that you are an American and you can speak
a little Chinese.
   a. **Wǒ shì Měiguó rén, bùdǒng yìdiǎnr hànyǔ.**
   b. **Wǒ shì Měiguó rén, dǒng yìdiǎnr hànyǔ.**
   c. **Wǒ shì Měiguó rén, hěn dǒng hànyǔ.**

7. You need help. So you approach someone and say:
   a. **Wǒ yào nǐ bāng wǒ.**
   b. **Tíngxià. Nǐ kéyǐ bāng wǒ ma?**
   c. **Duìbuqǐ. Nǐ kéyǐ bāng wǒ ma?**

8. You want to rent a minivan. You tell the clerk:
   a. **Wǒ xiǎng zū yí liàng miànbāochē.**
   b. **Wǒ xiǎng zū yí liàng xiǎo chē.**
   c. **Wǒ xiǎng zū yí liàng dà chē.**

9. At the service station you ask the attendant to check the
water and oil.
   a. **Jiǎnchá yíxià jīyóu hé shuǐ.**
   b. **Qǐng nǐ bāng wǒ jiǎnchá yíxià jīyóu, hǎoma?**
   c. **Qǐng nǐ bāng wǒ jiǎnchá yíxià jīyóu hé shuǐ, hǎoma?**

10. You want to know today's weather. So you might say:
   a. **Jīntiān tiānqì zěnmeyàng?**
   b. **Wǒ xǐhuān jīntiān de tiānqì.**
   c. **Nǐ xǐhuān jīntiānde tiānqì ma?**

11. You are asking the campground employee if there are essential
services. You would say:
   a. **Zhèr yǒu shùxǐjiān hé yǐnyòng shuǐ ma?**
   b. **Shùxǐjiān hé yǐnyòng shuǐ hěn guì ma?**
   c. **Wǒ xūyào shùxǐjiān hé yǐnyòng shuǐ.**

ANSWERS

Situation 3   3. a   4. b   5. a   6. b   7. c   8. a   9. c   10. a   11. a

177

12. You are asking the stewardess if they serve meals during the flight. You say:

    a. **Nǐmen chī fàn le ma?**

    b. **Nǐmen gěi fàn wǒmen chī ma?**

    c. **Nǐmen gōngyìng fànshí ma?**

Situation 4: Yúlè

Entertainment

1. Can you invite your business acquaintance to a movie this evening?

    a. **Wǒmen jīnwǎn qù kàn xì ba.**

    b. **Wǒmen jīnwǎn qù kàn Jīngxì ba.**

    c. **Wǒmen jīnwǎn qù kàn diànyǐng ba.**

2. Tell the hotel clerk that you like to jog in the morning.

    a. **Wǒ bùxǐhuān zǎoshang pǎobù.**

    b. **Wǒ xǐhuān wǎnshang pǎobù.**

    c. **Wǒ xǐhuān zǎoshang pǎobù.**

Situation 5: Diǎncài

Ordering a Meal

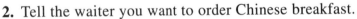

1. Ask your partner what he/she wants for breakfast.

    a. **Nǐ xiǎng chī zǎofàn ma?**

    b. **Nǐ chī le zǎofàn ma?**

    c. **Nǐ zǎofàn xiǎng chī shénme?**

2. Tell the waiter you want to order Chinese breakfast.

    a. **Wǒ xiǎng chī Zhōngshì zǎofàn.**

    b. **Wǒ xiǎng chī xīshì zǎocān.**

    c. **Wǒ xiǎng chī zhōngguóde fàn.**

3. Ask for a copy of the menu to look at. You would *not* say:

    a. **Qǐng gěi wǒ yíge càidān.**

    b. **Shàng càidān.**

    c. **Qǐng bǎ càidān gěi wǒ.**

ANSWERS			
Situation 3 12. c	Situation 4 1. c 2. c	Situation 5 1. a 2. a 3. b	

4. Ask the waitress for today's special.
   a. **Jīntiānde tècài shì shénme?**
   b. **Jīntiānde yǒu shénme hǎocài?**
   c. **Jīntiānde shénme hǎochī?**

5. You want to order tofu. You say,
   a. **Wǒ yào yìpán dòufu.**
   b. **Nǐmen zuò dòufu ma?**
   c. **Nǐmen de dòufu hǎo chī ma?**

6. You tell the waiter you don't drink wine.
   You want Chinese tea.
   a. **Qǐng gěi wǒ yìbēi jiǔ.**
   b. **Wǒ bùhē jiǔ. Qǐng gěi wǒ yìbēi Zhōngguó chá.**
   c. **Wǒ bùhē chá. Qǐng gěi wǒ yìbēi kělè.**

7. Ask the waiter what they have for dessert.
   a. **Nǐmen yǒu qiǎokèlì dàngāo ma?**
   b. **Nǐmen yǒu tiándiǎn ma?**
   c. **Nǐmen yǒu shéme tiándiǎn?**

8. You want to freshen up and want to know where the
   restroom is. You would *not* say:
   a. **Nǐmen zhèr yǒu cèsuǒ ma?**
   b. **Nǐmen zhèlǐ shì cèsuǒ ma?**
   c. **Qǐngwèn, cèsuǒ zài nǎr?**

Situation 6: Zài Shāngdiàn

At the Store

1. You've made your way to the store with the sign
   Fúzhuāng. What items will you *not* find there?
   a. **chènyī, biànkù, nèikù**
   b. **máoyī, dàyī, lǐfú**
   c. **zhàoxiàngjī, diànchí, jiāojuǎn**

2. Ask the salesperson if your companion can try
   on the suit.
   a. **Tā kéyǐ shìchuān yíxià ma?**
   b. **Wǒ kéyǐ shìchuān yíxià ma?**
   c. **Wǒmen kéyǐ shìchuān yíxià ma?**

ANSWERS

Situation 5   4.a   5.a   6.b   7.c   8.b   Situation 6   1.c   2.a

179

3. Now you're off to the **Ròudiàn.** Which list will you need for your shopping?
   a. **shūcài, shuǐguǒ, miànbāo**
   b. **tángguǒ, gāodiǎn, bīngqílín**
   c. **ròu, huǒtuǐ, xiāngcháng**

4. You're at the **Kāfēidiàn.** Which would you most likely get there?
   a. **yìbēi chá**
   b. **yìbēi kāfēi**
   c. **yìpíng píjiǔ**

5. Which of the following can you purchase at the **Yàodiàn**?
   a. **yào, kàngsuānjì, kàngjūnjì**
   b. **xiézi, píxuē, shǒutào**
   c. **diàoyúgān, kāisāizuàn, guō**

6. You've come down with a headache. You are at the **Yàodiàn** and tell the clerk:
   a. **Wǒ xūyào yìdiǎn zhì tóutòng de yào.**
   b. **Wǒ xūyào yìdiǎn zhì wèitòng de yào.**
   c. **Wǒ xūyào yìdiǎn zhì fùxiè de yào.**

7. You are asking the person at the laundry to remove a stain on your shirt.
   a. **Nǐ néng bǎ wǒde chènyī sòngqù gānxǐ ma?**
   b. **Nǐ néng chúdiào wǒ chènyī shàngde wūdiǎn ma?**
   c. **Nǐ néng bǔbu wǒde chènyī ma?**

8. At the barber's you tell the barber you want to have a haircut and a shave. You say:
   a. **Wǒ xiǎng xǐtóufa hé guāhúzi.**
   b. **Wǒ xiǎng guāhúzi.**
   c. **Wǒ xiǎng jiǎntóufà hé guāhúzi.**

Right place

Tāmen yīnggāi qù (They should go to)

1. _____ **mǎi** (to buy) **miànbāo.**
2. _____ **mǎi** (to buy) **xiāngbīnjiǔ.**
3. _____ **mǎi** (to buy) **shūcài hé shuǐguǒ.**
4. _____ **mǎi** (to buy) **niúròu hé zhūròu.**
5. _____ **mǎi** (to buy) **dàngāo.**
6. _____ **mǎi** (to buy) **kāfēi, chá, hé qìshuǐ.**
7. _____ **mǎi** (to buy) **yīfu.**
8. _____ **mǎi** (to buy) **xiàngliàn, jièzhi, hé ěrhuán.**
9. _____ **mǎi** (to buy) **jìniànpǐn.**
10. _____ **kàn** (to see) **xìjù.**

Situation 7: Bìyàode Fúwùjīgòu

Essential Services

1. You need some more cash for souvenir shopping.
   You go to the **Yínháng.**
   a. **Wǒ xiǎng cún yìdiǎn qián.**
   b. **Wǒ yào mǎi yì zhāng lǚxíngzhīpiào.**
   c. **Wǒ xūyào duìhuàn yìdiǎn xiànjīn.**

2. Can you find out today's exchange rate?
   a. **Jīntiānde duìhuàn lù shì duōshǎo?**
   b. **Jīntiān duìhuàn le duōshǎo?**
   c. **Shénme shì jīntiānde duìhuàn lù?**

3. You are telling the operator that you want to call collect.
   a. **Jiēxiànyuán, wǒ xiǎng dǎ yíge guójì chángtú diànhuà.**
   b. **Jiēxiànyuán, wǒ xiǎng dǎ yíge duìfāng fùkuǎnde diànhuà.**
   c. **Jiēxiànyuán, wǒ xiǎng dǎ yíge chángtú diànhuà.**

4. Ask your new friend for his telephone number in Chinese.
   a. **Nǐde diànhuà hàomǎ shì duōshǎo?**
   b. **Wǒ kéyǐ jièyòng yíxià nǐde diànhuà ma?**
   c. **Nǐde dìqūhào shì duōshǎo?**

5. You answer a call with:
   a. **Zài jiàn.**
   b. **Nǐ hǎo.**
   c. **Wèi!**

6. Tell the doctor that your throat hurts.
   a. **Wǒde hóulóng hěn hóng.**
   b. **Wǒde hóulóng hěn dà.**
   c. **Wǒde hóulóng hěn tòng.**

7. The dentist asks you to show where it hurts. You reply:
   a. **Wǒde hóulóng hěn tòng.**
   b. **Shì zhè kē yá tòng.**
   c. **Wǒde wèitòng.**

8. You feel sick and need to go to a hospital. You say to the hotel staff:
   a. **Sòng wǒ qù yīyuàn ba!**
   b. **Qǐng yīshēng lái!**
   c. **Sòng wǒ qù yàodiàn ba!**

9. If you are in danger, you would shout:
   a. **Láirénna!**
   b. **Bāngbang wǒ ba!**
   c. **Qǐng bāng wǒ!**

10. To express "Thank you," which of the following would you *not* say?
   a. **Xièxie.**
   b. **Fēicháng gǎnxiè nǐ.**
   c. **Búkèqi.**